The Mental Edge
~Revised

by

Loren Christensen

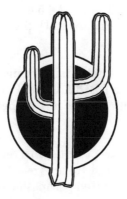

Desert Publications
El Dorado, AR 71730

The
Mental Edge, Revised

By

Loren Christensen

© 1999 by Loren Christensen

Published by Desert Publications
215 S. Washington
El Dorado, AR 71731-1751
870-862-2077

ISBN 0-87947-188-3
10 11 9 8 7 6 5 4 3 2 1
Printed in U. S. A.

Desert Publication is a division of
The DELTA GROUP, Ltd.
Direct all inquiries & orders to the above address.

WARNING

The author and publisher assume no responsibility for any liability, injuries or damages arising out of any person's attemp to employ any of the techniques described in this book; nor is it hte intent of the author or publisher to advocate the practicing of any techniques described in this book where those techniques may constitute any form of illegality.

ABOUT THE AUTHOR

Loren W. Christensen has been studying the martial arts since 1965. Over the years he has earned ten black belts, seven in karate, two in jujitsu, and one in arnis. As a karate competitor, he won more than 50 trophies in the black belt division.

His many articles have appeared in all the martial arts magazines, and he is featured in the book Who's Who in the American Teacher's Association of the Martial Arts. This is his tenth book about the martial arts.

You can visit Loren's web page at http://www.aracnet.com/~lwc123/

ACKNOWLEDGMENTS

Special thanks to my friend Laura G. Whited and my daughter, Amy Christensen for their work behind the camera.

Posing for pictures is always a pain, so I want to say thanks to my wife, Donna Duff-Christensen, friend and senior student, Mark Whited, stepdaughter, Kelly Henderson, students Jimmy Clarke and Jim Allan, and my son, DanChristensen.

Thanks to psychologist, Dr. Alexis Artwohl, with whom I wrote Deadly Force Encounters, for proofing the chapter, Fear.

Contents

INTRODUCTION

For years I have heard various martial arts instructors pretend to know what they are talking about when they have an audience at a party or, worse yet, when they are addressing their students. Their babble usually goes something like this. "You must become one with the four winds and flow with the yin and the yang. You must move with the speed of Buddha's breath, find the center of your being and flow to the outer universe as you fly with the eagles."

Oh-kaaaaay. So, what the heck does that mean? I don't have the foggiest idea. Do you? I know a lot of instructors who pretend they do, and too many students who are too intimidated to ask. This is ridiculous.

I'm not the sharpest tack on the wall (too many head kicks will do that to you), so I need something simple and something that works. This book contains the mental techniques I have found to be the most effective in my teaching, writing, personal training, and in real-life application during my long career in law enforcement. Although I've used the techniques for many years now, I'm still impressed and sometimes amazed at how well they work. Even more of a thrill to me is when a student enthusiastically praises their benefits.

If I may bore you for a couple of minutes, let me briefly tell you of my history in the martial arts, so you will know how I came to realize the benefits of the mind in my training, competing and thrashing around on the street with some seriously major human mutants.

I began training in the martial arts in 1965, and I think my progression in the fighting arts has been somewhat typical of someone with my longevity. During the first several years of training, my emphasis was on learning and developing techniques. By the time I earned my first black belt in 1970, I had spent a lot of time perfecting my power, speed, proper body mechanics, and accuracy of delivering techniques.

After earning my coveted belt, I trained for several years to develop my discipline even more. I wanted a will so strong that nothing could prevent me from reaching my goals, no matter what obstacles got in the way. I decided to do it through high-repetition practice, and I practiced zillions of reps. I remember some workouts so strenuous that my legs literally gave out and my arms ached and twitched so much I couldn't sleep. But I didn't let that stop me. No matter how sore, injured or sick, I would continue to set high-rep goals, often unrealistically. There were times when I was standing before a mirror and whipping out a thousand backfists, or working my way around a high school track thrusting out hundreds of sidekicks, that I wondered what the hell I was doing. Why was I putting myself through this agony? But I would continue, ignoring the pain and digging deeply into myself to bring out a little more energy and a little more strength. Although I didn't know how I was able to physically and mentally stand up the intense training, my ability to do so amazed me. How much more could I do, I wondered, if I actually understood what I was doing?

I decided to investigate the power of the mind further. I researched everything I could find about the application of mental skills to physical performance, especially books and magazines on the mental training of our Olympic champions. I talked with hypnotists, acupuncturists, physical therapists, marathon runners, champion bodybuilders, competitive skiers and masters of the martial arts. I was surprised in the beginning to discover a definite similarity in the mental training among all of these disciplines. Later as I became more aware of how the mind can be used, I realized that certain mental skills are basic to any physical effort that relies on speed, power and coordination of the mind and body.

They worked for me, they work for my students, and now I want to share them with anyone else who wants to improve. This book contains simple and easy to understand techniques that will bring out the best that you can be. You will learn how to think yourself faster, braver, tougher, and how to resist the temptations of skipping your training to channel surf through the boob tube.

I hope you will find this book to be a highly readable one, short on psycho babble jargon, and long on easy-to-use tools to make you the martial artist you long to be. I don't understand those ten dollar words, anyway. I like the ten cent words because they are simple and direct, and simple and direct is what fighting should be.

I learned in my 29 years of arresting people who didn't want to be arrested, that fighting is fast, furious and explosive, too much so for complicated, fancy smancy techniques. Since you should train as you fight, your training should be simple and direct. This includes your mental training.

I'm not a psychologist or a hypnotist, only a simple martial artist who began training in 1965, and had the good fortune to learn some valuable mental techniques that have been invaluable to me and my students. I have used these techniques for years and unfortunately have forgotten where I learned some of them. I apologize in advance if I can't give credit where credit is due. When I do know, I provide you with the source so you can research further if you so choose.

A word on the writing. There is a huge variety of martial arts systems and styles out there, but to make the writing easy, I use "karate" when referring to the kick/punch arts and "grappling" when referring to the wrestling-type fighting arts. I apologize if I offend anyone.

I'm also aware that both women and men train in the fighting arts. However, to avoid the awkward "he/she" word, I use the journalistically acceptable "he." Again, I hope this doesn't offend.

Be Mentally Relaxed

In a few pages, we will discuss self-hypnosis and mental imagery, both powerful tools that will dramatically help in your martial arts progress. But unless your mind is calm and relaxed, you won't be able to practice and benefit from them. Here is an analogy.

Toss a stone into a churning, pounding sea, and watch the rock sink with little if any visible effect on the surface of the water. But the stone is tossed into a clear, calm lake, you can easily hear the "ku-thunk," see the splash, and a series of spreading ripples. Your mind is like the ocean and the lake. If it's agitated, your efforts to create growth-producing mental imagery or to give your mind self-hypnotic suggestions will be in vain.

Additionally, you can't train, compete or defend yourself when your mind is tense and your body is tight. Overall, your techniques will lack speed, explosiveness, flexibility and strength. When your mind is tense, you will have a hard time perceiving, reacting and adapting to your opponent. Think of tension as a mental blockade that prevents your body from performing at its best.

Weight training as a supplement to your martial arts training is great. In fact, I think students who train with weights have an advantage over those who don't. It's been my experience, though, that hardcore lifters, especially bodybuilders, have a tendency to flex their muscles while executing their techniques. This is

Be Mentally Relaxed

probably because they are conscious of their development and believe they must show their strength by flexing. Wrong.

When lifters tense their muscles, their biceps may bulge, but their martial arts movements suffer. This is because movement, especially fast movement, requires a sharp contraction of the muscle fibers in the limb doing the technique. For example, those muscles involved in throwing a backfist are the upper back, shoulders, upper arm and the muscles surrounding the elbow joint.

To launch the backfist with speed, your muscle fibers must contract violently. But if they are already contracted– tensed– there isn't much left for them to do since they are already doing it. If say, 80 percent of the fibers are already in a contracted state before the backfist is launched, the result will be a slow, stiff backfist strike.

You also get tired faster when your muscles are tight and flexed. Physical tension in the martial arts, often comes with mental tension, which adds up to dissipated energy and exhausted muscles. Your legs will be heavy, your reflexes slow, and your lungs will burn. Not an ideal condition to be at your best.

Mental Tension
This is the day and age of industrial strength stress. You don't have to be a hardcore bodybuilder to have tense, tight muscles,

Work, bills, family problems and not enough hours in the day add up to a stressed life.

3

because when you are mentally tense, whether from everyday stress, or any number of other causes, your muscles will react the same. No matter what the cause of the tension, the end result will be slow, ineffective techniques.

The antidote to tension, no matter where it comes from, is relaxation. When you learn to turn relaxation on, so to speak, you will be able to think more clearly, have greater control over emotions like anxiety, fear and anger, and deliver your techniques with greater power and speed. You will be the master of yourself and the situation.

As you practice the following exercises once a day, you will happily discover that it becomes more and more easy to bring on the relaxed mental and physical condition. You will reap the benefits of it in your everyday life, as well as in your martial arts training.

Besides fighting better and as a preparation to the mental imagery and self-hypnosis exercises, there is one other benefit of learning to relax: It just feels darn good. When you learn to bring it on at will, it's as if you are being enveloped in a warm, comfortable blanket. Pretty cool. And it doesn't cost a thing.

THE EXERCISES

There are lots of exercises out there, but I have narrowed down my personal list to just three, settling on these after eliminating others that, for whatever reason, didn't work for me. Also, these easy-to-do exercises have been popular with other people, too. Each one is quite different from the others, so there is a good variety to try.

Typically, it takes a few sessions to get the feel for a relaxation exercise, so don't discard one until you have tried it several times over a period of a week or two. You don't want to toss out an exercise prematurely that could possibly be the most beneficial one, if only you had given it enough time to find out.

You may choose to stay with one exercise, because you find that your mind responds to the consistency of using the same one each session. Or, you may prefer to have several to choose from, finding that your mind responds differently on different days. It doesn't matter as long as it works for you. When you

4

have found the method that suits you, do it two or three times a day until you are entirely comfortable with it. Practice your exercises in a quiet, comfortable place, totally void of all distractions. Remember, once you are comfortable bringing on a relaxed state, you will be ready to try self-hypnosis and the mental imagery exercises.

Now that I've said that you need to have quiet and comfort to bring on the relaxed state, let me say that it's possible to bring on a "shallow level" of relaxation in places that are not quiet and serene. For example, if I'm in a stressful situation, whether it's a martial arts situation or one in some other area

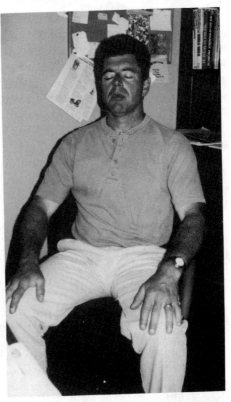

Even at work you can bring on deep relaxation by getting comfortable and using whatever inducement method you prefer.

of my life, I will concentrate on my breathing to bring on instant calm to my mind and body. I have done this unnoticed while in a crowded room, while waiting to give an important presentation, and while driving my car. The depth of my relaxation is not as profound as when I do it in the quiet of my home, but it's sufficient to satisfy my need at the moment.

The first time I realized I could get the benefits of relaxation without lying down in a quiet environment was when I was facing an angry mob in my job as a police officer. I had been called to a demonstration where about 150 people were trying to get into a building where one of our senators had an office. The crowd was made up of two groups of people with opposing political views, and as always happens when the police arrive, both groups joined forces to fight us. There was lots of pushing and screaming and several arrests were made. At one point, I found myself blocking a door to the building while the crowd screamed and threatened me. I felt a little like General Custer must have felt at his last fight. I was breathing as if I had been running sprints, my eyes were watering and my hands were trembling. This was definitely not the quiet, peaceful setting I was used to, but I nevertheless began a slow, ryhthmic breathing pattern. I kept my eyes on the crowd, though I was aware of the cooling, calming oxygen being drawn deeply into my belly. I held it there for a moment, then I slowly let it out my nose. I did this so subtly that not one of the angry demonstrators knew what was going on. Within moments, I was calmed, relaxed and able to control myself and the dangerous situation.

The bottom line of this anecdote is that the more you practice relaxation, the easier it becomes and the more comfortable you are doing it in places other than in an ideal environment.

Do the following formal exercises whenever you want to experience the benefits of deep relaxation, and whenever you are preparing for the self-hypnosis and mental imagery exercises described later.

The Position

The following is to be used no matter what relaxation method you choose to do. Your place should be comfortable, quiet, and with a pleasant temperature so you can wear light, loose-fitting clothes. If you choose a bed, or sofa, it needs to be supportive and have a place to rest your head on a small pillow. If you have low back problems, you may want to place a pillow under your knees. Allow your hands to rest comfortably on your lower abdomen and refrain from crossing your legs. If you fall asleep easily lying down, use a seated position that is comfortable and offers good support. Rest your hands in your lap or on your knees.

Let your body sink heavily into whatever you are sitting or lying on, and slowly close your eyes. Breathe in through your nose, drawing the air slowly and deeply into your lower belly. If your chest expands, you are not breathing correctly. You want the air to expand your belly on each inhalation.

Drawing the air should take about six seconds, then hold it for about three seconds, and then exhale for another six. The entire process should take about 15 seconds.

Don't force your breath; there should be no strain in this procedure. If you feel your inhalation is complete at three seconds, that's fine. But strive to make it six seconds in and six seconds out. After practicing the exchange a few times, you will naturally time your breathing correctly.

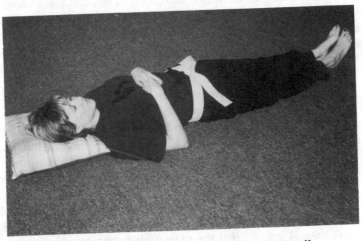

Getting deeply relaxed prior to training will greatly improve your workout and your ability to learn.

Blue Fog

After a few deep breath exchanges, you will begin to feel a mild calming effect throughout your body. To enhance this, imagine the incoming air as a cool, blue fog that enters through your nose, and swirls down your lungs into your belly, thighs and feet. As you hold the blue fog in place for three seconds, picture it tumbling about your body, cooling and calming it. Then slowly exhale, imagining the fog reversing the route and flowing out your nostrils, though now it's red from all the collected negative elements in your body, like fatigue, tension, anger, and frustration. As you release these poisons with each exhalation, sink deeper and allow yourself to become more and more relaxed.

Progressive Muscle Relaxation
Bruce Lee liked this method.

Get comfy on the floor, your bed or in your favorite chair, and repeat as many deep inhalations and exhalations as it takes to bring on relaxation and to get settled into your position.

As the name suggests, you are going to progressively and systematically relax your body, beginning with your feet, then your calves, thighs, buttocks, abdomen, chest, arms, shoulders, neck, and face. Your objective is to tense and relax each major body part until you are completely bathed in a sensation of warm relaxation. The word "bathe" is a good descriptive word, because the sensation is just as if you had submerged yourself in a delightful tub of warm water.

Here is how you do progressive relaxation.

Move your thoughts to your feet. See and feel them in your mind, your toes, your arches and your heels. Now, tense them hard for five seconds and then abruptly stop the muscle tension. Inhale deeply, and then exhale slowly as you feel the pleasurable, soothing sensation of your feet sinking deeply into the surface of whatever they are resting on.

Direct your mind to your calves, and mentally feel every inch of them. Now, tense them hard for five seconds, and then abruptly relax them. Can you feel the pleasurable sensation that permeates the muscles? Take a deep breath into your belly, and exhale as you allow your lower legs to sink deeply into the surface of whatever they are resting on. Caution: Be aware that the calf muscles are susceptible to painful cramping when doing the tensing portion of this exercise. If this happens, stop the tension and concentrate on relaxing the muscle group.

Now let's move on to the thighs and repeat this same process, and continue through all the muscles groups up to the face. As you did with your feet and calves, begin with awareness, then contraction, abrupt relaxation, and a deep breath to sink the body part into whatever it's resting on. You may want to subdivide your body parts down further, especially if you are not getting as relaxed as you want. For example, subdivide your arms into hands, forearms and upper arms. You can break your back (so to speak) into lower and upper.

Tense a body part for five seconds (some people do ten seconds), and then relax it for five to ten seconds before moving on to the next one. Continue to breathe slowly and deeply throughout the entire process.

After you have moved from head to toe, take a few minutes to enjoy the sensation of total relaxation as you inhale and exhale deeply. Mentally scan your body to see if there is a part that needs to relax further. If your thighs need more, put your mind on them and allow them to sink more deeply each time you exhale.

Neutral Bath

You will find that neutral bath is an easy way to get relaxed, is highly pleasurable, and a method that can be practiced every day, unless you're the kind of person who bathes only on Saturday night. You need a warm bathroom and a bathtub filled with warm water. A hot tub works, too, as long as you don't have the water too hot. When you submerge yourself into warm water, you will quickly be lulled into a relaxed state where you can enjoy the sensation for its own sake, or use it to ready yourself for mental imagery practice or self-hypnosis.

The reason neutral bath works is because your skin surface is covered with sensitive nerve endings that react to stimulus. Most of these are cold receptors, and when water that is colder than your body makes contact with them, you feel the difference. The greater the difference between the temperature of the water and that of your body, the greater the potential for a physiological reaction, such as shivering, goose bumps, and shock. On the other hand, water that is the same temperature as your body will have a soothing effect on the nerve receptors and your overall nervous system. So effective is it that years ago, before tranquilizers were developed, a neutral bath was used to calm agitated patients.

Try it at the end of a hectic day. Get an inexpensive thermometer at any pharmacy to ensure that the water stays between 92 and 96 degrees the entire time you are submerged. You don't want cool air on your body, so keep the air temperature in your bathroom sufficiently high.

You will experience a wonderful sedative effect that will relax your muscles and begin to calm your mind. When you incorporate your breathing exercises, you will be reduced to a mellow piece of Jell-O. I like to do the progressive relaxation exercises while I'm in my hot tub, finding that it takes me to a deep level of relaxation.

Although you may choose to have a neutral bath every day, you should never have one prior to a workout since it will drain your energy.

Six-Gate Breathing

An acupuncturist taught me this Chinese method of achieving deep relaxation several years ago, and it has remained one of my favorites ever since. Six-Gate Breathing refers to six entrance and exit points on your body where breath is exchanged: the palms, the bottoms of the feet, the navel and the nose. Of course, you really can't breathe through your hands, feet and naval (or can you?), so you must visualize the process at those points. If this seems silly to you, bear with me and give it a chance.

Get into a comfortable position, lying or sitting, and then close your eyes. Slowly inhale, visualizing the air (make it blue fog if that helps you see it better) swirling through the bottoms of your feet, tumbling up through your calves, thighs, abdomen, chest, arms, neck and into your head. Your inhalation should be slow and steady until your entire body is filled. Take a moment to see and feel the fog as it calms and relaxes your body. Then as you exhale through the bottoms of your feet, imagine the fog having turned red from the collected tension and fatigue. See it tumbling downward from your head to join the fog that is moving up from your hands and arms. From there, it joins the fog in your chest as it passes through your abdomen, pelvis, thighs, calves and out through your feet. Your exhalation should be slow and steady until the fog is completely out of your body.

Now you are going to breathe through the palms of your hands. Inhale and visualize the fog entering through them, moving up your arms, then filling your head, chest, abdomen, and legs. When your body is saturated, pause for a few seconds to enjoy the calming sensation, then, beginning with your feet, reverse the order as you exhale the fog back out your palms.

Next, you are going to breathe through your naval. Visualize inhaling through it, letting the fog fill your lower abdomen and then flow over into upper half and lower half of your body. To exhale, simply reverse the process.

Lastly, you will breathe through your nose. Draw the air in slowly, and picture the fog swirling downward to fill all of your body. Reverse the process when you exhale.

There are teachers who recommend that you inhale through your nose and exhale out your mouth when practicing any of the breathing exercises. Other teachers suggest inhaling and exhaling through your nose. I don't see any difference. Try both and see which you prefer.

Key Word

Key word is a nifty device that quickly and easily gets you started into a state of relaxation. I feel that it's so effective and beneficial that it's easily worth the price of this book (which you got at a ridiculously low price, anyway). Choose any word you like, such as 'relax," "calm," "tension go." I use my middle name, Wayne. It works well for me because I don't know anyone named Wayne, I seldom hear it, and I use only my initial when I write my name. And best of all, I can remember it.

First, you need to develop a comfortable level of expertise with one or more of the relaxation methods just discussed. When you are deeply relaxed and susceptible to autosuggestion (see Self-Hypnosis, Chapter Three), tell yourself that whenever you say the word "relax," or whatever word you choose, you will immediately experience a sense of deep relaxation wash over you. You may have to tell yourself this for several sessions until it takes hold in your subconscious mind. Even after it's working for you, you should give yourself the command once a week to ensure that it remains entrenched.

Since it's not necessary to lie down and close your eyes to benefit from your keyword, I've used mine while riding in a car, on an airplane, while sitting backstage preparing to give a talk, and while waiting to compete in a tournament. Simply sit still for a moment, take a couple of deep breaths and whisper the word so that only you can hear it. You will immediately enjoy a pleasant sensation of relaxation.

I use my keyword for two purposes: to bring on a mild sense of relaxation to better enjoy my day, my training, or to better perform at a given task. The second reason is to give myself a jumpstart into the relaxation process for self-hypnosis or mental imagery.

● ● ● ● ●

No matter if you always use the same method to achieve deep relaxation, or you choose a different method each time, the benefits of relaxation will help you physically and mentally. A relaxed mind thinks more clearly and perceives at a faster rate. A relaxed body can more easily respond to the rigors of training, competing and fighting for real.

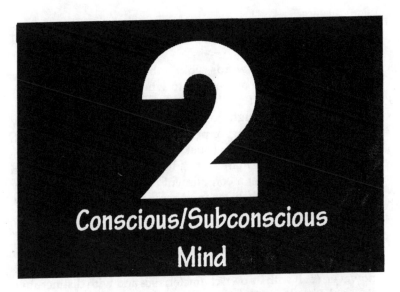

2

Conscious/Subconscious Mind

I've got a sign in my school that reads "CAN'T Is A Four-Letter Word. " Yes, it sounds like a bumper sticker, but don't shrug it off as insignificant. Its meaning is as simple as it is profound, one that is extremely important to your martial arts success as well as your success in other areas of your life.

When I hear a student say something like "I can't get this kick," or "I can't do my kata very well," I jab my thumb at the sign and tell them to watch their language." If you are having trouble with something," I say sternly,

Consider "can't" to be a four-letter word in your training.

"ask for help like this, 'Could I have help with this kick?' or 'What can I do to improve my kata?'"

I make an issue out of not saying those two little words because they are extremely powerful and can negatively affect your training, progress, competition and survival in a knock-down drag-out. This is because every time you say "I can't," there is another part of you listening– your subconscious mind. Even if you just whisper the words, your subconscious is eavesdropping and nodding in agreement to whatever you say. It never argues; it just agrees. (Wouldn't it be nice to be married to someone like that?) Although you may be just kidding about how bad you are at something, or perhaps digging for a compliment, when you say, "My sparring sucks," your subconscious is nonetheless listening. As smart as it is, it can't differentiate between words said just to get a compliment or said because you truly believe them. It simply listens and accepts literally what it hears.

DO YOU HAVE TWO MINDS?

You may have two stomachs, one for dinner and one for desert, but you have only one mind. There are two parts to it, however, each with its own characteristics and with distinct abilities and functions. These two parts go by several names, like "waking mind," and "sleeping mind." But for our purposes here, we will call them by their most common names: the conscious mind, which deals with the world you live in every day, and the subconscious mind, which deals with the vast, uncharted world within yourself.

You reason with your conscious mind, and you use it to analyze, doubt, guess, wonder, calculate and assimilate. Just like a sieve, everything soaks through it after it filters out what it doesn't want. Everything you see, hear, feel, touch, and smell is recorded in the form of mental pictures and then passed on to your inner, or subconscious mind where it is filed away for future reference sort of like a computer.

It chooses things, too, like this book it so wisely selected, that cup of coffee you just sloshed onto your fingers, and that chair you are slumped in. All choices are made with the conscious mind as it guides and directs your daily life. The conscious mind has no creative power. It has only the duty of sending its reactions and thoughts on matters to your subconscious. Your subconscious mind accepts everything you imprint on it as true and then goes about bringing that truth back to you in the form of your actions. Using the earlier example, if you think and say often enough that you cannot spar well, your subconscious mind will believe you and make sure that you can't.

14

Understanding this simple fact is extremely important to your martial arts success. You must be constantly aware of what is going on in your conscious mind so that your subconscious is being fed data that is positive, happy, constructive, peaceful and so on. If you have been filling your mind and speech with "I can't," and other negatives, you need to take steps right now to change this pattern to enable your subconscious to guide you in a positive way. You must train your conscious mind to act as a security guard against negative data entering and being sent on to your impressionable subconscious.

Always remember that your subconscious doesn't analyze the information it receives; it only accepts it literally and then acts on it.

She Did What She Said She Would Do

I had a student who was an excellent technician in kata. Her techniques were razor sharp, her form was flawless, and she delivered her moves with power and speed. While training for an upcoming tournament, however, she continually blanked out on the same technique, a jump kick that occurred about three quarters of the way through the 100-move kata. Each time she executed the jump, her mind screeched to a stop, and she could not remember what came afterwards. When I would remind her, she would always get angry at herself for a second, and then finish the kata without further problems.

I had her practice that portion of the kata over and over until she could proceed all the way through without freezing. Two days before the tournament, her kata looked great, and I felt confident that she would blow her competition out of the water.

When the big day came, she was worried about having a relapse of her earlier problem. "I just know I'm going to freeze after the jump," she said. "I can just feel it."

I talked to her at length, trying to get her to *believe* that her kata was in the best shape it had ever been in, and that she would dazzle the judges. But the closer the time came for her to compete, the more negative she became. "I'm going to blow it. I'm going to be so embarrassed," she said, convincing herself that she was going to fail.

Which she did.

Don't let negative thoughts affect your kata performance.

She saluted sharply when the judges called her name, and began her kata with her characteristic explosive block/punch combination. She then proceeded through technique after technique until she got to the jump kick, which she executed flawlessly. Then she froze, as a flush of red spread across her blank face. A moment later she shook her head, bowed to the judges, and left the ring. Later, the head judge told me she would have captured first place if she hadn't stopped dead in the water.

While I was disappointed I wasn't a bit surprised, since she had told herself verbally and in her thoughts that she was going to fail. Her subconscious simply accepted this input as gospel, in spite of the fact that she had performed the kata marvelously for the past several days. Unknowingly, she gave her subconscious mind direction to make her freeze after the jump kick. Of course she didn't want to embarrass herself in front of all those people, but she nevertheless set herself up for it.

The subconscious mind is absolutely incredible. All that you have heard and seen is recorded there. People under hypnosis have regressed back in their lives to when they were three months old. That's right, three months. They have been able to accurately describe their crib, the pictures on the wall, the design of the wallpaper, and even conversations that took place between people in the room. Of course, they didn't understand what they were seeing or hearing at that age, but since it was recorded in their subconscious, they were able to translate it years later when they were adults.

In the pages that follow, you will learn how to tap into your subconscious mind to help you progress in the martial arts. Using relaxation exercises, self-hypnosis, affirmation and mental imagery, you will learn to program your subconscious mind to accept positive data, which will then direct your body to perform positively.

The Mental Edge
Edge
~Revised

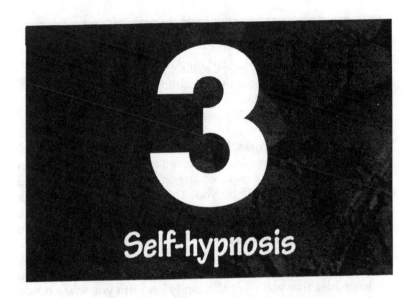

3
Self-hypnosis

The word hypnosis often conjures images from old movies or carnival side shows where the "victim" is seen walking about in a trance, arms extended, or crawling on all-fours and barking like a dog for the amusement of a studio audience. Well, that's exactly what you are going to be doing here. Just kidding.

What you will be doing, after you have gotten deeply relaxed from one of the methods you learned earlier, is giving yourself powerful suggestions that will dramatically help your martial arts.

The word "hypnosis" comes from the name of the Greek god of sleep, *Hypnosis*, first used by an English physician, Dr. James Baird in the mid 1800's. The word can be a little misleading because hypnosis has nothing to do with sleep. It's actually a deep state of relaxation in which there is an increased ability of the mind to receive suggestions. Hetero hypnosis refers to the type that is brought on by another person called a hypnotist. Auto-hypnosis, also called self-hypnosis, means that the condition is induced by one's self. We will only be examining self-hypnosis here, but if you are so inclined, you might want to check out a hypnotist for further study.

There is nothing mystical about self-hypnosis, but it's amazing how it helps your martial arts, such as in the following ways.

* Enhances your ability to learn
* Erases fears and self-doubts

* Improves your physical skills
* Improves your competitive abilities
* Breaks bad habits
* Improves your ability to relax

Here is how it works. We are all susceptible to suggestion, whether it comes from another person or from ourselves. When you practice self-hypnosis, the suggestions come from you, to you, and are heard only by you. The old saying "You can talk yourself into or out of anything" is what self-hypnosis is all about, and when you do it in a specific way for a specific objective, you can reap incredible results.

Unknowingly, our minds are constantly being stimulated by suggestions from powerful outside sources. For example, you had no idea that you wanted a candy bar until you saw a candy display rack by the grocery store cash register. And you didn't realize what a junker you drove until you saw that shiny red sports car down at Bing's Used Cars. Powerful suggestions of all sorts bombard our minds all day long.

Self-hypnosis is even more powerful. The difference, however, is that you are in control of the input, you are deciding what specific, positive thought you want entering your subconscious mind. As already, mentioned, there is nothing mysterious about all this, because it's based on the natural relationship between the conscious and subconscious mind. With your understanding of how easily this works, your martial arts will improve in wondrous ways.

HOW IT'S DONE

If this procedure seems a little involved, don't be put off; it will become quite easy after you have done it a few times. Like other areas in your martial arts study, the more you practice, the easier the effort will become, and the greater your benefits.

Know What You Want

The first step in the process of self-hypnosis is to know what it is you want to improve. In order to have a clear picture of your objectives, form a list of all the things you want to accomplish in your martial arts study. Consider the following.

* I want more confidence for tournament competition
* I want to improve my sparring
* I want to improve my kata
* I want more self-discipline
* I want to earn a black belt

Your list might look similar to this or it may contain different objectives. What is important is that you carefully analyze yourself and create a list specific to *your* needs and wants.

Give yourself suggestions to improve your sparring.

First, get relaxed

To induce self-hypnosis, you must first get into a state of deep relaxation. Choose one of the methods illustrated in Chapter One and bring on the soothing calm of deep relaxation. As you do the procedure, feel all your tensions melt away, and feel your body grow heavier and heavier as you sink lower and lower into relaxation. Some people call this sensation "letting go," which is a good term for the sensation. You will feel as if you are bordering on sleep, but your mind will be alert, and your subconscious will be ready to receive your powerful suggestions.

Don't take shortcuts with the relaxation process in your eagerness to get to the self-hypnosis procedure. It's rather like a block and counter in karate: If you don't block the assailant's attack, you are not going to get off your counter punch. Likewise, if you don't get yourself deeply relaxed, you are not going to benefit from self-hypnosis. Your body and mind must be in a state of deep relaxation to be receptive to the suggestions.

The Eyelid Test

Once you are in a deep state of relaxation, you want to test yourself to determine how receptive you are to the power of hypnotic suggestion. It's a simple test that uses your conscious mind to tell your subconscious mind to close your eyes and keep them closed.

Begin by fixing your eyes on a small object directly to your front and at eye level, perhaps a tack on the wall or a pattern in the wall paper. The following are some of the suggestions I use when doing the eye test. You don't need to memorize them. They are presented here to give you an idea of the wording and the process, so you can develop your own. You can say them in the quiet of your mind, or if you are having trouble concentrating you can mouth them silently, or whisper them softly.

"Now that I am deeply relaxed, I am going to slowly count to ten and my eyelids will grow heavy, watery and tired. My eyes may even want to close before I complete my count to ten. When they close, I will be in a hypnotic state. I will be fully conscious, hear everything, and be able to give suggestions to my subconscious mind."

"One . . . my eyelids are becoming heavy . . . two . . . My eyes are becoming watery . . . three . . . My eyelids are growing tired and heavy . . . four . . . I can hardly keep my eyes open . . . five . . . My eyes are beginning to close . . . six . . . my eyes are so very heavy . . . seven . . . I am deeply relaxed . . . eight . . . I can't keep my eyelids open . . . nine . . . My eyelids are closed . . . I am in a self-hypnotic state . . . ten . . . I am now susceptible to whatever post-hypnotic suggestion I want."

These suggestions should be made slowly and with pauses between each so that your mind has time to absorb them. Take your time and repeat some of them if necessary. Remember to maintain your deep, rhythmic breathing throughout the entire session. For example, pause after "I cannot keep my eyelids open," so you can do three or four repetitions of deep breathing, as your eyes close lower and lower.

The Tingling Hand Test

Here is another test you can do to ensure that you are relaxed and open to suggestibility. I prefer this one because I'm never absolutely sure that my eyelids are closing involuntarily. With the tingling hand test, the sensation is so intense that it leaves no doubt that you have reached a suggestible state. To conduct the test, start your dialog from the point where you have sunk into deep relaxation.

"I am completely relaxed . . . As I slowly count to ten and even before I get to ten, I will experience a tingling sensation or a sensation of numbness in my right hand . . . One . . . I am concentrating on my right hand . . . I can see it in my mind . . . it is completely relaxed . . . Two . . . I am beginning to feel a pleasant tingling sensation in my hand . . . Three . . . I can see my hand in my mind's eye . . . It is relaxed . . . limp . . . heavy . . . relaxed . . . Four . . . I am relaxed . . . Five . . . My hand is beginning to tingle . . . tingle . . . tingle . . . Six . . . It's a pleasant feeling . . . I am relaxed . . . I feel heavy . . . My hand is tingling . . . Seven . . . It's tingling more now . . . It's becoming stronger . . . Eight . . . It's an enjoyable sensation . . . Nine . . . It's really tingling now . . . tingling . . . Ten . . . I am now in a hypnotic state and susceptible to suggestions. (Whew! I got sleepy just typing that.)

If your mind is receptive to suggestions, your eyelids will close or your hand will tingle. If it doesn't happen the first time, don't get over concerned. The next time you try, make sure you are completely relaxed and concentrating as intensely as you can on what you are doing. You must believe that it will happen. You must tell yourself over and over that it will happen. Remember, the name of the game here is autosuggestion.

Don't be concerned about your eyelids staying closed forever or your hand tingling until you are 95 years old. Both conditions will end when you come out of your hypnotic state. Once your eyelids have closed, you may continue with other hypnotic suggestions, but if you used the hand tingling test, you must stop the sensation so you are not distracted. Here is what you say to stop the tingling.

"The tingling in my hand will go away . . . My hand will return to normal . . . I realize I have reached a deep hypnotic state . . . My entire body is relaxed . . . every muscle . . . I like the sensation . . . The tingling in my hand has stopped . . . I am now ready to give suggestions to my subconscious mind."

Improving Your Martial Arts With Self-Hypnosis

Look at the list you made earlier about what you want to improve in your martial arts. Prioritize it so that the first item you want to work on is at the top. The first item on my list is, "I want more confidence for tournament competition."

Do you see how I made this statement a positive one? By stating it as such, I am already on my way to thinking positively. No matter if you are frightened to death of competing, you never want to discuss it, write about it, or even think of it in negative terms. When you say, write, or think, "I am afraid of competing," you release negative energy and negative memories of tournament experiences you have had. Even if you have never been in one, but you are terrified of your first, your negative thinking will reinforce your fears.

I'm going to flame this so it sticks in your mind. IT'S PARAMOUNT TO YOUR SUCCESS THAT EVERYTHING YOU SAY, THINK AND WRITE ABOUT YOUR GOAL IS POSITIVE AND DIRECTED TOWARD IMPROVEMENT. More on this in a moment.

Here is one other important aspect of self-hypnosis. Although you may have several items on your list, your mind will be at its best working with just one at a time. Since tournament competition involves kata, sparring, judging, demonstrations, and belt promotion, you must narrow this item to just tournament fighting. First, concentrate only on improving one thing, in this case it's confidence for tournament fighting. A few days later, you can add another element of tournament competition to work on.

Analyzing Your Objective

So far, you have picked your objective, which you have reduced to a positive statement, and you have broken it down so that you are dealing only with one element of it. Now you are ready to analyze it through self-hypnosis to determine how you feel about tournament fighting.

Use your favorite method to induce deep relaxation, and then test your susceptibility by using the eyelid test or the tingling hand test. When you feel you are ready, give yourself the suggestion that you are going to analyze your feelings toward tournament sparring. You will ask yourself a series of questions and allow your brain to analyze your subconscious mind while it's in a clear and relaxed state.

* What are my feelings about getting hurt?
* What are my feelings about being embarrassed in front of others?
* What are my feelings toward specific competitors?
* What are my feelings toward competing in front of an audience?
* What are my feelings toward losing?
* What are my feelings toward winning?
* What are my feelings toward my physical condition?
* What are my feelings toward putting my reputation on the line?

You're a pretty tough interviewer, huh?

Be aware that your conscious mind may not know all the answers and, even if it does, it may not always be honest with you. Many of the truths have been buried in your subconscious mind

25

for many years, and will only come out as you analyze yourself in the self-induced hypnotic state. On the other hand, you might be amazed at the honesty of the answers and perhaps even a little shocked. You may not like every thing you hear, but at least the answers are out in the open (at least in the privacy of your own mind) where you can more easily deal with them.

Analyze one question at a time and try to come up with as many answers as you can. Take your time to mull the questions and answers around in your subconscious mind, as you discuss them with yourself in order to see every angle, and to examine everything that bubbles to the surface. Sometimes a thought will appear that seems ridiculous. Don't toss it out too soon, because after you give it consideration, it just might end up being a significant part of your problem as well as your solution.

As mentioned before, there is nothing mystical about this process. It's all based on natural functions of your brain. It's really fun and quite satisfying. It's like that wonderful feeling you get when you connect with a person in deep conversation, except this conversation is with the greatest person in the world– you.

After you have awakened from your self-hypnotic state, write down everything that came to the surface of your mind. In one section of your log, write down the problems you found. In another section, write down any solutions you discovered, things you are going to do to improve yourself. The act of writing helps to solidify your thinking and provides a quick reference to an organized plan of correction.

Through self-hypnosis and the listing of your findings and solutions, your mind is on its way toward improvement. Get ready to improve even more.

Use Only Positive Suggestions
As mentioned before, when you continuously convince yourself that you can't do something or you are not good at something, your subconscious mind will direct your actions to prove yourself right. Your physical limitations aside, many of the problems that you have listed are probably a result of your subconscious mind feeding your conscious mind negativity. The good news is that you can change this.

After you have analyzed your problem during your self-hypnosis session, you are ready to begin programming your mind toward making a positive change. This is done by giving yourself positive suggestions to replace the negative ones you have been feeding it your entire life. It's sort of like you have a video tape in your head on which you have recorded an old movie. You are tired of it now, and you want to replace it with something new– something much, much better.

Let's say that one of the major issues you discovered during your analysis was that you have an intense anxiety about performing in front of crowds. You list this discovery in your notebook, and in your solution column you write suggestions that are positive, such as the ones I have listed below. Take special note of the italicized words that give power and color to the suggestions. The word might seem to be an exaggeration, but that's OK because you want them to charge you subconscious with positive energy.

* I *love* fighting in front of crowds.
* I use a crowd's presence as a source of *dynamic* energy that gives me *awesome* strength and *blinding* speed.
* My *thunderous* punches and *pile-driving* kicks will *thrill* the crowd.
* I will *learn* from my errors because they are part of the *tremendous* growth I am experiencing.
* My body is filled with an *electrically-charged* energy that will *ignite* the crowd, create *thrilling excitement* and bring *riotous* cheers.
* I will think of the nervous butterflies in my stomach as charging me with *stupendous* energy and anticipation to get into the ring.
* I am a *performer*, a *showman*, and a *warrior*, ready to *thrill* the audience with the *beauty* and *razor-sharp precision* of my techniques.

Highly descriptive words will communicate intense, emotional feelings and greatly influence your subconscious mind.

It is also mandatory that your suggestions are in the present tense since the subconscious has trouble dealing with the past

Tell yourself that you love to perform in front of a crowd.

and future. Don't say, "Next week at the tournament when I'm preparing to fight . . ." Instead say, "As I prepare to fight, the butterflies in my stomach are flitting about charging me with great energy and anxious anticipation." Always make your statements in the present, even though you are preparing for something in the future.

Copying Over The Old Tapes

Now you are going to imprint these positive suggestions into your subconscious, that is, erase the old negative tape in there and replace it with a positive, highly charged one.

Induce deep relaxation, test yourself with the eyelid or hand test, and then begin to give yourself positive suggestions. Take your time with this. Pause between the suggestions to breathe in deeply and exhale slowly as your powerful words etch themselves into your subconscious. Enjoy the relaxed sensation that has enveloped your body. Repeat often that you are relaxed, calm and receptive to the suggestions. Don't just say empty words, but *feel* their meaning. It's important to listen and understand what you are saying. Repeat sentences if you wish, especially if your mind wanders for a moment.

Most often I *think* the suggestions, but if I'm having trouble concentrating, I mouth them silently or, if I'm having a lot of trouble staying focused, I'll whisper them. Hearing the suggestions helps me get focused.

Developing Confidence

Perhaps you joined a martial arts school for the same reason many people do, to develop self-confidence. Self-hypnosis can be used to build an attitude of internal strength into your subconscious, so that your daily training and competition are met with positiveness, rather than self-doubts. When you have entrenched a strong, positive mental attitude, your body will relax and your true potential will come through. Your improved technique will in turn reinforce the power of your suggestions to have greater confidence, which creates a circle, resulting in you growing stronger mentally and physically. Here are some examples of suggestions that will help you develop self-confidence.

As usual, you will say these things after you have induced a deep state of relaxation and tested yourself to see if you are receptive to suggestions.

"I have been training hard and I'm prepared for competition (or class). My reflexes are razor sharp, my blocks are lightning quick and my footwork is evasive and explosive. My punches are like dynamite and my kicks are laser-fast. I'm as good as I can be at this point in my training, and I am as good as anyone in my division (or class). I'm learning from this experience and enjoying it to the utmost. I'm ready and eager for the moment."

Don't Program To Win

Although making positive suggestions to your subconscious mind programs you to be your best and creates a winning attitude, you should refrain from giving yourself suggestions to win. This can cause confusion in your mind when an opponent scores on you or when you lose a competition. Think of your mind as a computer. If you program it only with the suggestion to win, but you are scored on five times in a row and lose your first match, your programming is going to be confused. This isn't a good thing for your confidence. It's better to create suggestions that you fight at your best, and that you consider getting scored on as a positive learning experience. Here is how you should suggest this.

"I'm learning from my mistakes. I know that if he scores on me, I will need to do a better job of covering my openings with my guard. If he scores on me, I will remain confident and strong. I know that his hitting me and my hitting him is part of the sparring experience. I'm blocking my best. I'm fighting as well as I can, but if he scores on me, I will learn from the experience and grow as a fighter."

By making these suggestions, you can get hit, but you continue fighting because you consider it a learning experience. Imagine how disastrous a street fight would be if you only programmed yourself to win. When the attacker hit you, you would be so mentally disrupted that he could easily defeat you before you could recover.

There are schools where students never make contact in their drills or in their sparring. By training this way, they program their subconscious not to expect physical contact when fighting. Unfortunately, some students achieve high belt rank training like this. But a problem arises when they spar someone from another school who likes to make contact, or when they get into a street fight and get hit by their assailant. It's not uncommon for these students to freeze in shock when they get hit, even when hit lightly. If it happens on the street, a second of hesitancy can get you killed.

Don't set yourself up to be shocked. Instead, give yourself suggestions like the following that will help you develop a powerful winning attitude.

"I feel energy when I train and compete. I'm a winner because I am participating. I'm a winner because I'm gaining experience that will help me progress. I'm a winner because I'm continuously learning. Even if my opponent gets more points, I'm a winner because I participated and learned from the experience."

With these suggestions, you create a winning attitude that comes from the experience of having participated in the training, competing and learning. If you do win a trophy, consider it a cherry on the pudding since you are already a winner in your mind.

Programing Techniques

You can program your mind to respond to specific attacks right in the comfort of your own easy chair.

"When my opponent lifts his leg to roundhouse kick, I quickly angle away and counter with a blistering-fast sidekick to his midsection."

Or, "I respond to his hand attack with an explosive front kick to his groin."

Or, "I am throwing two or three backfists to my opponent's face, and just as he thinks I am going to do it again, I slam a hard roundhouse kick into his middle."

These are excellent suggestions to get you countering more effectively. You may know how to deliver the techniques, but your mind is not yet programed to let you react to an attack with a fast counter attack. These autosuggestions will get you on the right track.

31

Visualize your opponent chambering his leg to roundhouse kick.

and then see yourself sidestepping the chambered leg and landing a side kick.

Enhanced Learning

Using self-hypnosis is an excellent way to prepare you to be receptive to material that you find technically difficult. Self-hypnosis will clear your mind for the learning and give you confidence to do your best.

The ancient art of tai chi incorporates slow, rhythmical movements that serve as exercise, a sort of moving meditation, and as a subtle but effective method of self-defense. Learning the forms and executing them requires that you use every bit of your concentration. When I was studying the art, I would arrive at my class about 20 minutes early to give myself time to mentally prepare. I would remain in my car, get into a comfortable position, then induce relaxation. After I felt that warm, wonderful sensation sweep over me, I would give myself suggestions to be receptive to the intricate patterns I would be learning. I would say the following.

"Tai chi is easy to learn. I am highly receptive to the learning. I'm listening to all that my teacher has to say, and I easily absorb the instruction. I'm relaxed, my movements are soft and flowing, like a leaf blowing in the wind. This is my best class ever."

I used suggestions that relaxed my body and prepared my mind to be receptive to learning. Since tai chi uses movements that are soft and flowing, I wanted to be as relaxed and calm as possible. This usually took me about 20 minutes to achieve, after which I would go into the class receptive for the material.

On those days when I was rushed and harried and didn't have time to perform my self-hypnosis, my classes were always more difficult. My mind would flutter all over the place, and my muscles would do everything but the right thing.

Awakening From Self-Hypnosis

When you have finished your statements, you will want to tell yourself that on the count of five, you will return to a fully awakened state. "In a moment, I am going to count slowly backwards from five to one, and on the count of one, I will awaken refreshed, alert and responsive to all the suggestions I just gave myself. Five ... I am beginning to awaken ... Four ... I am awakening ... Three ... My eyes are opening ... two ... My eyes are open ... One ... I am fully awake, refreshed and ready to carry out my suggestions."

After you return to your normal consciousness, take a few moments to sit quietly and enjoy the feeling of peace that has enveloped you. You may have a feeling of lightness, as if your arms could drift upward. There is a clarity and calmness in your mind and you have fewer rambling thoughts bouncing about. It's a wonderful feeling, and you should take time to enjoy it.

While Driving
You must be careful with this.

I have found that a mild form of self-hypnosis can be done while driving to class or a tournament. It's mild in the sense that I'm fully awake and driving my car, as compared to a deeper form of self-hypnosis where I lie down and close my eyes. This is how I do it.

As I'm driving along, I induce a pleasant sense of relaxation by doing slow, deep breathing as I concentrate on making my muscles feel light and my mind clutter free. I go only for light relaxation, NEVER deep relaxation. I tell myself that although I am becoming relaxed, I'm still alert and aware of my driving responsibilities. I repeat this to myself several times. I then proceed with my positive suggestions about where I am going, which could be my class, a competition or a talk.

To repeat, my inducement is light and superficial since I'm driving. Still, I get a lot out of it.

A word of caution: DO NOT PRACTICE SELF-HYPNOSIS WHILE DRIVING IF YOU ARE AT ALL TIRED, SLEEPY, OR HAVE EVER FALLEN ASLEEP EASILY DURING A SELF-HYPNOSIS SESSION.

● ● ● ● ●

There are people who think that self-hypnosis is weird or something to be feared. People who believe this way are simply uninformed, usually because they have gotten their information from the movies. To correct these false beliefs, all you have to do is try it. It doesn't take more than two or three sessions to realize how natural, fun, relaxing and remarkably beneficial it is.

The Mental Edge

~Revised

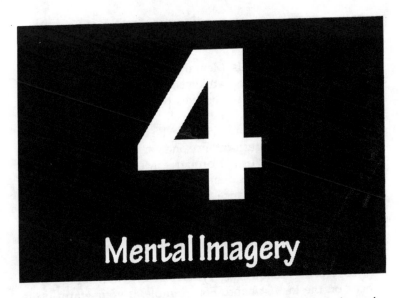

Mental Imagery

Whether you think you can, or whether you think you can't, you're right. - Henry Ford

Mental imagery is also called visualization and sweatless practice. For our purposes here, mental imagery is the process of imagining yourself performing a specific activity in your art. You see yourself performing flawlessly and with success, whether your scenario is in your school, tournament, or fighting in the street. You create the imagery with all of your senses so that you see, hear, feel, touch, and even smell all that is involved.

Does it work? Oh yes. I tell my students that if there is indeed a secret in the martial arts, it's the practice of mental imagery. It's simple yet highly effective. Once you get into it and discover how effective it is, you will kick yourself for not having used it sooner.

Here are some of the things you can use it for.

* To see your success: Many martial artists "see" themselves achieving their goals on a regular basis.
* To motivate yourself: It's difficult to be hungry all of the time. Using mental imagery before your training sessions, such as calling up images of your goals for that session, can remind you of your objective, and get you motivated to train hard.

* To perfect your skills: Mental imagery can help you learn and refine your skills. Top athletes in other fields use mental imagery to see and feel themselves performing perfect skills, programs, and routines.

* To entrench: Mental imagery can be used to entrench sparring techniques, kata performance and confidence.

* To set the stage for performance: Mental imagery can be used for pre-competition planning to help you set the mental stage for a good performance. Many top athletes do a complete mental runthrough of the key elements of their performance to bring out their desired pre-competition feelings and focus. This also helps keep negative thoughts from interfering with a positive pre-game focus.

* To refocus: Mental imagery can be useful in helping you to refocus on the task at hand. For example, if your warm-up is feeling sluggish, mental imagery of a previous best training session or competition can help get things back on track.

Mental imagery has been around for a long time and used by athletes for a long time. It's only been in the past two decades, however, that it's gotten public recognition. Consider golfing great, Jack Nicklaus, who has used mental imagery for years. He says, "I never hit a shot even in practice without having a sharp, in-focus picture of it in my head. It's like a color movie. First, I "see" the ball where I want it to finish, nice and white and sitting up high on the bright green grass. Then the scene quickly changes, and I "see" the ball going there: its path, trajectory, and shape, even its behavior on landing. Then there's a sort of fade-out, and the next scene shows me making the kind of swing that will turn the previous images into reality. Only at the end of this short, private Hollywood spectacular, do I select a club and step up to the ball."

Many Olympic athletes say they use mental imagery, and that they devote a big part of their training to visualizing gymnastic routines, weight lifting, downhill ski runs, archery, high jumping or whatever their event is. They use it because they know that it's an effective, easy-to-do exercise that often makes the difference between winning and losing their event.

Studies have been conducted using basketball players, dart board competitors, and other people who engage in sports that require precision skill. The studies separated the people into three groups: those who physically practiced every day, those who didn't practice at all, and those who used only mental imagery. After several weeks the groups were tested. As you might expect, those who didn't train didn't improve, but the groups that only rehearsed their skills mentally improved nearly as much as the ones that physically practiced.

I first heard of mental imagery over 20 years ago at a seminar conducted by Chuck Norris. He says that when he was competing and knew that he had to fight a particular competitor for the first time, he would watch the man during his earlier matches to see how he moved and responded. Norris would then find a quiet place where he could conjure mental imagery of his pending fight. He would see the man's roundhouse kick, see himself block or evade, and then see himself counter with a clean, point-winning technique. He said that he would mentally create a variety of exchanges, where he would always see himself scoring with the winning point.

When Norris actually climbed into the ring, he said he felt that he had a distinct advantage, because he had "experience" fighting the man, though the man didn't have experience fighting him. Norris' attacks and counter attacks flowed just as he had visualized them, and he made every winning point that he had seen in his mental practice. Chuck Norris used mental imagery for all of his competitive years and retired as Middleweight Champion of the World.

SWEATLESS PRACTICE

As mentioned, mental imagery is sometimes called sweatless practice, a good name since you can do the exercise right in the comfort of your easy chair without having to change into your workout clothes and raise a sweat. It's serious practice, because even though you are only visualizing your effort, you are benefitting almost as much as when you do the exercise physically. Here is how you do it.

Get Relaxed

As we have been saying all along, your mind is most receptive when you are physically and mentally relaxed. When you are going about your daily business at work or school, and your mind is otherwise busy and occupied, your brain is in a place called beta level. But when your grey matter is enjoying deep relaxation, your brain wave pattern becomes slower and moves into a place called alpha level. You want to be in alpha level when you do your mental imagery and self-hypnosis exercises.

Many people find that one of the best times to relax is in the morning upon arising or just before going to sleep at night. Your mind is highly receptive during these times because in the morning your mind has just rested, and at night your mind is preparing to rest. If you fall asleep easily during these times, do your relaxation exercise sitting up in bed or in a comfortable chair, and make sure that your back is straight. Researches have found that a straight spine helps bring on the alpha level condition.

Or Don't Relax First

OK, now that you understand that relaxation brings on the alpha state, a condition where your mind is highly susceptible to suggestions and mental imagery, I'm going to tell you that you don't always have to get relaxed. Here is what I'm talking about.

You now know that mental imagery exercises work best when you are in a deep state of relaxation. But if you are in a situation where you can't or you don't have time to induce deep relaxation, you can still benefit from mental imagery. I have practiced it while sitting in a boring meeting, while watching television, while standing in line at the grocery store, and while parked at the curb watching passersby. I'll simply do a little deep breathing to bring on a mild state of relaxation, and then without closing my eyes, I'll imagine my activity. Of course, this isn't as good as when I'm in a quiet place and have taken the time to get into alpha state, but I nonetheless still benefit from the mental repetitions.

Here's How

Let's do a practice run with this incredibly easy exercise using your front kick. After you have induced deep relaxation, see yourself standing in your fighting stance, lifting your rear leg and chambering your knee near your chest. Your arms are in the on-guard position as your leg thrusts forward until it's fully extended. See your leg retract, again chambering near your chest, and then your foot returning to the floor.

Pretty easy. Did you make your images as clear and vivid as a TV screen, or were they more of an impression or a feeling of the kicking action? You should strive for a clear image, though some people can only bring forth an impression or a feeling of the action. If this is your way, that's OK. What is important is that you are doing the activity in your mind.

Visualize In Real Time

A big mistake I made early on when using mental imagery was visualizing an activity at a slower speed than I would do it for real. I would take 10 minutes to progress through a 90-second kata. This is wrong. You must see yourself doing the action at reality speed. If your backfist and reverse punch combination takes a half second to do, then that is how long you should visualize it.

Some people find that at real speed it's hard to bring in all the details of the technique that are so important. Other people say it's easier, because when they visualize slowly they have a tendency to lose their concentration. If you find it difficult, just keep on practicing until you get it.

Your Best Performance

This time you are going to do your best kata, reliving the time you performed it better than at any other time. It may have happened in your backyard, in your school, or in competition. It doesn't matter if you won or lost the tournament or if other people thought it wasn't your best. What is important is that you thought it was because all the elements were there for you–speed, power, precision, mental attitude, and that wonderful feeling when you know you are hot.

Get relaxed and prepare to see in your mind that great kata performance once again. It's important to bring to your image every detail about the moment, such as the feel of your uniform,

Visualize your best performance and bring to the image all that was good about it.

the snap of your punches, the crispness of your kicks, the speed of your movements, your sense of drama, and the feel of being in a real battle. If people complimented you after your real-life performance, hear those comments again. If the crowd cheered, hear it again. Put every aspect of that positive experience into your mental imagery, and practice it over and over to embed it into your subconscious mind.

This time visualize your sparring. Again choose a time when your sparring was right on the money– in class, in competition, even in a real situation– and bring that experience into your mind. Don't visualize the entire session, just the highlights, those moments when your punches, kicks and blocks were working 100 percent for you. Create mental images of how you set the techniques up, the stances used, the hand techniques that got in, the kicks that hit their targets, and the way you moved defensively.

Mental imagery is a great way to bring back those moments when everything went well for you. Not only do you have the fun of reminiscing about a time when you were at your best, but through mental imagery, you can imprint into your mind the physical, mental and emotional experience from that great day.

Decapitate Your Hero

This is an interesting approach to mental imagery that you will find fun as well as beneficial. The concept is to swap heads with someone whose techniques you admire. Here is how it works.

Say you like your instructor's flawless and effortless jujitsu techniques. Or perhaps you like the way a fellow student launches a picture-perfect sidekick/back kick combination. By forming a perfect mental image, you will become that person you admire and perform your movements as precisely as he performs them. Let's do your friend's combination.

Get relaxed and deep into alpha level, so that your mind is receptive to the images you are going to put there. There are two methods of head swapping; experiment with both and see which you prefer.

With the first, you superimpose your good-looking face over his so that his face and head dissolves, and your face and your

Visualize your head on the shoulders of someone whose technique you admire.

entire head suddenly appears atop his shoulders as he stands in his fighting stance. Hold this image as you watch yourself perform his beautiful sidekick/turning back kick combination.

The second method of head swapping is to see your friend's technique as if you were looking out through his eyes. Choose your favorite method and repeat it often as you like.

Details, Details, Details

Not only do you want to recall those techniques you used to trash your opponent at the last tournament, but you want

44

to involve as many other detaisl as you can. It's good that you can recall that charging front kick/ridge hand combination that earned you the winning point, but you also want to bring as many sensory sensations as possible.

Remember the sound of the cheering crowd and your supportive teammates. See their clapping hands, their pumping fists in the air, their smiling and laughing faces. Recall how your ridge hand felt as it sliced through your opponent's guard and smacked against his neck. Let the energy of that beautifully executed technique fill your muscles as you sit or lie in a position of deep relaxation.

Reach into your memory and bring forth as many sightss, sounds and smells as you can. You are playing a movie that is in a film canister in your head. See it with all its details.

Grappling

Whether you practice jujitsu, judo, police defensive tactics, aikido or a karate style that uses a lot of grappling techniques, you will find that mental imagery is a wonderful tool to embed into your mind the intricacies of grappling techniques.

When I was preparing for my second-degree black belt exam in jujitsu, mental imagery made up about 50 percent of my training time. My situation was such that I had a hard time getting training partners to help me prepare, so mental imagery became my partner, one that allowed me to do anything I wanted without having to listen to him complain.

I broke my training into three sections: mental imagery, pantomiming, and practicing with live opponents. The mental imagery portion I practiced after inducing deep relaxation and at other times when I only mildly relaxed myself. I liked the mental imagery practice because I could do it often, and I never had to drive anywhere or change my clothes. Pantomiming practice I did at home or in my school after all the students had left. Although I physically did the moves, it was also a form of a mental imagery, because I practiced seeing and feeling my opponent's reaction.

I found that when I practiced with live opponents, my technique was just as sharp as it would have been if I had been practicing with them all along. The only change was that I had to adjust to having a real body and real weight to deal with.

I passed the test with flying colors.

A Marriage Of Mental Imagery And Self-Hypnosis

Did you notice that the process of mental imagery and self-hypnosis is similar? You begin by inducing deep relaxation, using one of the methods you learned earlier. You test yourself with the eyelid or hand tingling test, then you proceed with either the autosuggestion or mental imagery. Here is a way you can kill two birds with one stone by combining self-hypnosis and mental imagery to prepare for a belt test.

If you are like a lot of students, you probably suffer from "test anxiety." Your instructor has scheduled a belt examination in a couple of weeks, so you have a case of the butterflies and sweaty palms that just won't quit. Although your techniques are ready, the idea of demonstrating your stuff in front of your classmates and instructor absolutely terrifies you. Your nerves are shot.

Test anxiety is a problem not just limited to testing in the martial arts. Perhaps you experience these same feelings in your regular school or on your job. There are probably lots of reasons why your confidence goes south before a test, some of which could be traced back to early experiences in your schooling. Why this happens is not your immediate concern here. You just want to do something to reduce the anxiety so that you can perform at your optimum. Since the martial arts are instrumental in building self-confidence, you need to act now to take steps to rid yourself of those feelings and replace them with strong self-assurance. Here is the good news: It's easy to do.

First, bring on that wonderful feeling of deep relaxation and test yourself for suggestibility. Remember "keyword" we talked about in the Chapter Three, Self-Hypnosis? After you have induced relaxation, say the word, "confident," to yourself. This is a word you will eventually use to immediately bring on a sense of confidence before your test. Here is how you should talk to yourself.

"I'm *confident* and I'm ready for this examination. My techniques are strong, fast, and my form is perfect. I have trained hard and I have all the skills and knowledge necessary for the belt I want. I'm filled with the knowledge and *confidence* that I have the ability. I'm prepared and I'm *confident*. I'm ready and *confident* to face my instructor and show him and the other students what I have learned. As I walk to the center of the room, I'm filled with *confidence*. There is strength in my walk. My self-*confidence* radiates from my body and from my eyes. My every move is that of a winner. I'm standing proud and *confident*."

Don't rush through these suggestions. Emphasize the word, confident, as you say the suggestions slowly. Pause between the suggestions so you can reflect on each one. Repeat them until their meaning is clear in your mind. When you say something like, "there is strength and confidence in my walk," take a moment to feel what those words mean.

Your next step is to visualize your *confidence*. Say to yourself, "I'm now going to see myself confident and positive as I proceed through the test requirements. I see how well I'm performing; I see the *confidence* radiate from me; I see my every move done with self-assurance, precision, and strength."

Create a mental image of the setting where you will be and then put yourself smack in the middle of it. See yourself standing calmly, confident, and raring to go. Your hair is combed and your uniform is washed and pressed; you look sharp. See yourself radiating with certainty as to your ability to perform at your best. Hear your name called and see yourself walk to the front of the room with a confidence that practically shouts its authority. Feel the excitement pump through your veins, supplying you with confident energy, strength and speed. See yourself performing requirement after requirement with the knowledge that you have *already* passed the test. At the completion of the test, see yourself standing tall and proud as to how well you have performed. The judges can make only one decision: Pass.

At the completion of your self-hypnosis/mental imagery session, say the word "confident." Tell yourself that whenever you say the word prior to testing, or any other time you need to act with confidence, you will feel a sense of confidence surge through your body. Tell yourself this several times over several sessions so that it becomes imbedded into your subconscious. After a few days, you will be able to just say the word and get an instant replay of your visualized confidence. Continue with the formal sessions, but use the keyword as a way to bring on a shot of confidence whenever it's needed.

When I say the word, I inhale deeply then exhale slowly as I breathe out and enunciate every letter. C-o-n-f-i-d-e-n-c-e.

YOU CAN THINK YOURSELF FAST

I wrote a book a couple of years ago titled *Speed Training: How to Develop Your Maximum Speed for Martial Arts*, published by Paladin Press. Besides making a shameless plug here, I mention this to give an example of how powerful self-suggestion can be, even when you're not aware that you are doing it.

Speed Training took about eight months to write. I researched scientific documents, interviewed martial artists, searched through literally hundreds of martial arts magazines and dozens of books, to collect data on how to increase the speed of punches, kicks and blocks. Then I personally experimented with the myriad of concepts, principles, exercises, and drills that I found, and also taught them to my students so they could experiment with them. After only about three months of researching, compiling notes, thinking about speed, and all that is involved with it, I discovered I was getting PDQ, Pretty Darn Quick.

I've been blessed with fast hands from my very first day of karate, and cursed with slow kicks. Over the years of my training, I progressively improved my hand and kicking speed. It was about 15 years ago that I figured I had gotten about as fast as I would ever get, that I maxed out. After all, the human body does have its limitations. I compared it to building muscle: You can only get so big.

But suddenly, through no conscious effort of my own, I discovered that my hand techniques were getting faster and my so-so kicks were improving, too. How could this be? I wasn't complaining, you understand, I just couldn't figure out why it was happening. Then I started thinking about my research, in particular, something I heard repeated by a number of incredibly fast martial artists who I had interviewed and read about.

To paraphrase, this is what they said: You can THINK yourself faster.

Yes, you read that right. "You can think yourself faster." *Think.* Wow, that beats getting all sweaty.

I had been so preoccupied with speed– hand, foot, blocking, offense, defense - that I was unconsciously imprinting in my mind that I was getting faster. For example, when I compiled a list of drills to improve the speed of the backfist technique, I saw myself doing them and thought about them improving my backfist. When I compiled a number of techniques, drills and concepts to add zip to the roundhouse kick, I envisioned those things improving my own kick. Is this mystical or supernatural? Not at all. Let's put it in a different context.

If you have ever considered owning a red, convertible sports car, how did you envision yourself in it? For sure you didn't see yourself being ignored by the opposite sex or looking like a big, geek loser behind the wheel. You probably saw yourself wearing designer sunglasses, looking cool and suave, and cruising low and slow while the opposite sex stared at you with salivating hunger. You created a mental image of yourself that was positive and successful.

Well, that was what was happening when I was compiling information for the book. Although I didn't see myself wearing cool sunglasses and capturing admiring glances (well, perhaps a little), I did think a lot about getting faster. When I made notes and thought about the elements of a drill that would increase the speed and explosiveness of the backfist, I thought about my backfist. Whenever I thought about any method to improve speed– something I was preoccupied with for over half a year– I thought about my techniques. Unconsciously, I was putting into my subconscious the belief that I was getting faster. This was new information in my little brain because, as I mentioned earlier, 15 years earlier I had programmed myself to believe my speed had reached its peak.

Here is how this can work for you.

Believe that you can be faster. As mentioned throughout this book, *be positive*. Go into to your training, especially your speed drills, absolutely *convinced* that the training is going to make you faster. If it's a backfist drill, *believe* that yours is already fast and is going to improve even more. Be convinced that the exercises are going to work, and that you will soon be faster.

When you spar and when you work on your drills, even when the emphasis is not on speed, *act* as if you are fast. I'm not talking about showing off, but rather popping those punches, whipping in those roundhouse kicks as if you are the king or queen of speed.

Some speed experts believe that 90 percent of being fast is thinking you are fast. In my own experience, I would guess about 50 percent of my improved speed came from my belief. But whether it's 50 or 90, your positive belief system will make it work for you.

Self-doubt will hold you back, restrict you, and make your moves heavy and laborious. Confidence and a conviction in your mind that you are fast will direct your physical being to move with speed. Add to your belief system lots of good physical exercises, and you are on your way to being Pretty Darn Quick.

THINK LIKE A BAD GUY

Here is a fun exercise using mental imagery to teach yourself about the dangers of the street. You won't be going into a deep state of relaxation or using self-hypnosis, but you still will be using your imagination to visualize. It's a way you can be a crook without getting arrested or shot by a frightened victim. You will like this exercise (just don't like it too much and take off into a life of crime) because you will be departing from your law-abiding life to view your surroundings and passerby through the eyes of a thief, rapist, assailant, mugger or any other kind of law breaker you can conjure. You will see places to hide, to leap out from, to run to, and places to drag your screaming victims to do whatever you plan to do to them. And you will see victims, lots of helpless, delectable looking ones. Here's how it works.

Let's say you ride the bus home from school or work every day. You get off at the same corner and walk to your home or walk to a park-and-ride lot where you get into your private car. There is a woman who gets off the bus with you and always walks in the same direction. She is middle aged, in poor physical condition, her arms are always full of bags and packages, and she is oblivious to her surroundings. She's a perfect victim, and you are going to attack her.

First, you need to check out the environment to determine the best place and the best time to do the crime.

* You've noticed that she is friendly to people, so you can engage her in conversation to get her to lower her guard.

* She is always wearing a head set, so you know you can come up from behind without her hearing you.

*You can jump her when she passes by that big truck that's always parked in the same place, then drag her into the alleyway.

* You can thump her over the head as she passes by the doorway in that long-empty building on the corner.

You can hide behind this van and then jump out and grab this woman.

This is a great place to hide before you leap out and grab this woman's purse.

* You can leap out from your van that you parked at the corner, and pull her inside.
* Since she is walking next to the curb, you can stand between that Toyota and that Ford, then step out quickly and snatch her purse.
* You can hide behind the car that is parked next to where she always parks, and then leap out as she fumbles with her car keys.
* You can deliberately park your car near hers in the morning so you can easily confront her in the afternoon.

Let's change the setting to a picnic in a beautiful park, an example I chose because a policeman friend was stabbed recently while picnicking with his family. He survived, but barely. Look around at all the opportunities that await the lowlife criminal that you have become in your mind.

* Notice the expensive ice chest left unattended on that picnic table.
* You follow that five-year-old who has wandered off from her family.
* You hang around the brick restroom for whatever opportunity presents itself.
* You deliberately pick a fight with a guy who has consumed too many beers.
* You prowl the parking lot looking for cars where the owners have left windows down.
* You're a male and you approach a woman who is sunbathing in an isolated location.

Let's change the setting one last time to a shopping mall. Your exercise this time is to sit on a rest bench and see how many potential victims pass by.

* An old man teeters by and you notice his Rolex watch.
* A ten-year-old passes who appears to be alone at the mall.
* A blind woman passes, her white cane tapping on the floor.
* A wealthy-looking woman passes with her leather purse dangling from one hand, her other struggling with a Saks 5th Avenue package.

Thinking like a bad guy programs your mind to recognize certain patterns, signs and behaviors that cause people to become victims. Your objective is to see these things in those places that are common in your life, such as movie theaters, clubs, the parking lot behind your martial arts school, the supermarket, and so on. At first you will have to make a conscious effort to think like a bad guy and see all the potential around you, but in time, you will do it unconsciously, even in new places. You will quickly see those things that don't look right, and react to ensure your safety. From practicing this exercise, you will no longer perceive your environment as a whole, but rather see it in parts.

People who are victimized didn't see the danger because they were focused on the whole. Most often, the suspect is right there at the corner, lurking between those two parked cars, or following closely behind. But victims missed seeing the threat because their eyes and minds were not perceiving the specifics of their surroundings.

The police officer who patrols your neighborhood looks at the streets, sidewalks, parks, parking lots, alleyways, and school yards differently than you do. His unique experience there forces him to perceive people and places in a manner that helps him to protect you and himself. Unless you are a police officer, you will never see the world the same way he does, but by practicing looking at things through the eyes of a bad guy, you will expand your awareness and dramatically decrease the chance you will be taken by surprise.

Fear

Volumes have been written on the subject of fear, but for our purposes here, I have taken this huge subject and reduced it to one little chapter. What it contains, however, are devices that I have found helpful in my own growth in the fighting arts, and what I have taught others to use. For the average martial artist, the tips in this chapter will suffice, especially when they are coupled with the relaxation, self-hypnosis, and mental imagery exercises discussed in this book. If they are not, I encourage you to seek out further reading or help from a professional therapist. Psychologists and counselors have techniques that help dispel those fears that are extremely stubborn, or that derive from other issues, such as depression, anxiety and physical health.

I said earlier in this book that the journey you take in your study of the martial arts is called the "path" or the "way." The Chinese call it "tao" and the Japanese call it "do." By whatever name it's called, you will find, or you have already found, that it's a path littered with obstacles and traps that make your journey a tough one.

Most people, who decide to study martial arts, do so to overcome a common obstacle that has been hindering their path long before they ever walked into a jujitsu or karate school. I'm talking about fear. Their pride and machismo may keep them from admitting that they have fear, but the truth is that most martial arts students begin training in the hope of overcoming it by learning the physical skills necessary to defend themselves. This may not be enough, though.

If fear was your motivation to join a martial arts school, you may sadly discover that it's still there, consciously or subconsciously, no matter how advanced your belt level or how many trophies you win. Fear is not always as obvious as other obstacles, such as illness, broken bones, family commitment, financial woes and a host of other goodies that somehow always arise to turn a good day into a bad one. Nor is fear a tangible thing, like a flat tire that prevents you from making your class, or that cast on your wrist that has had you sidelined for a month. But fear can interfere with your progress and, if it gets out of hand, it can even cause you to regress.

There are three factors that comprise a fear situation. First, there is a feeling of danger, that is, there is something capable of causing you harm. Second, there is a feeling of vulnerability. You feel you can be harmed. And third, there is a belief that you are incapable of dealing with the danger. If you take a moment to analyze one or more of your fears, you will find at least one of these factors present.

We are going to look at two types of fear, one that is real and one that is manufactured. Real fear is a survival signal that announces itself only in the presence of danger, such as a guy charging you with a Samurai sword. Manufactured fear, which manifests itself in your imagination or comes from a past memory, can still have a powerful influence over you. While the cause of these two fears may be different, their symptoms are the same.

* Pounding heart
* Muscle tension
* Trembling
* Watering eyes
* Gut-wrenching knot
* Dry mouth
* Nausea

* Jumpy, easily startled
* Urge to use the bathroom
* Insensitivity to pain
* Rapid, shallow breathing
* Sweating
* Dizziness or light headed

56

Some of these changes are designed by nature to help you fight hard or run away as fast as you can. Others are side effects of chemicals dumping into your body that cause a high arousal state. One symptom that can be both good and bad is your insensitivity to pain. It can be good, in that you can fight without being distracted by blows that hit you, and it can be bad, in that you can get hurt but be unaware of how serious your injuries are until later when you are no longer aroused, a situation that could be fatal.

But when manufactured fear (sometimes called "worry") is left to brew, it becomes counterproductive to your ability to fight well. Since it's *created* in your mind, your imagination will distort reality, making an average-size tournament opponent appear to be a giant, fire-breathing dragon. As your imagination takes off, your confidence to deal with the tournament fighter, or any other situation where your mind has distorted reality, will leave you helpless. Your body will react by making it hard for you to breathe, your muscles will be drained of energy, and your reflexes will be slow.

Fear that is created in your imagination feeds on itself and creates a sort of circle. The negative physical reactions will affect your ability to fight, so that your opponent can easily score on you. This will psyche you negatively, making you feel even more vulnerable and incompetent, which again will negatively affect your fighting ability.

This spinning cycle of negativity will grow larger and larger. You will begin to lack confidence whenever you spar, whether it's in school or in competition. From there, you will begin to doubt your abilities as a martial artist, and if this really spins out of control, you will begin to develop a distorted view of yourself as a person. This cycle must be stopped if you are going to have a future in the martial arts and a healthy self-image.

Let's do two things here. First, let's look at how you can harness the symptoms of real fear to give yourself strength and speed. Then let's examine imagined fear to see how you can diminish it in your mind so that you can defend yourself, compete and train at your best.

UNDERSTAND AND ANTICIPATE
THE SYMPTOMS

Understanding what can happen, and knowing that it probably will happen, will go a long ways toward letting you to be comfortable with the symptoms. Know that fear symptoms are caused by biochemistry from the high-arousal state, and that they make you alert, and are a positive and powerful source of energy and strength to help you survive. You can get control of these reactions by practicing the controlled breathing and relaxation techniques described earlier. These exercises won't prevent the symptoms from happening, but they will help you control their intensity.

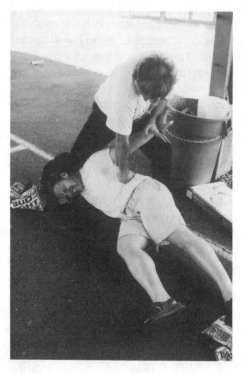

You can reduce the fear of a real fight by anticipating that it might happen.

Being in a real fight is scary, but you can reduce the symptoms of fear to some degree by anticipating that a fight might happen. All too often, martial arts students get caught up in belt promotions, tournament competition, and the social aspect of their school. This is fine, but the danger is that the concept of real fighting gets lost. Yes, the students are practicing fighting techniques, but they are not thinking in terms of *real* fighting. They are not thinking at all about the big difference between sparring for fun and having to defend against some lowlife who thrusts a knife at their face.

Acquiring The Physical Skills

Have fun in your school and in your competition, but think seriously about the reality of self defense. There is nothing more frightening than to suddenly discover that you are in a real fight and that what you have been practicing for the last couple years has been only for sport. I found this out the hard way when I found myself working as a military policeman in the very mean streets of Saigon, Vietnam. No matter what your friends or your teacher tells you, there is a big difference between tag karate and fighting for your life. If you haven't been in a real fight, talk to people who have. Analyze your training and insist that your instructor teaches realistic techniques. If he doesn't, move to a school that does.

The more you think about real fighting, the more you learn to keep your eyes open to the dangers around you (refer to "Think like a bad guy" in Chapter Four), the more you reduce the element of shock and the explosion of biochemical reactions that occur when fear strikes. Your response is dependent upon your physical and mental preparation toward having to save your bacon in a real fight.

Other things that can help you respond in a positive way are a healthy diet, sufficient sleep, not abusing alcohol, drugs, and caffeine, and being in good physical condition. The more physically fit and highly trained you are, the better you can cope with the sudden emotional and physical stress of a life-threatening self-defense situation.

BREAKING DOWN YOUR IMAGINARY FEAR

When a street thug steps out of a dark alleyway brandishing a knife, that flash of fear you feel will help you fight or run. However, fear that you create in your mind interrupts clear thinking, and is a waste of time and energy. Analyzing your manufactured fear through a process of breaking it down step by step will weaken its impact on you, because you will see it for what it really is. Since you probably generalize your feelings, the process of carefully analyzing them will bring out the specifics of your concern and, more times than not, allow you to see that there really isn't much there to be frightened of at all.

For example, you say that you are afraid of sparring John, a fellow classmate. Saying, "I'm afraid of sparring John," is a simple declaration of a general feeling that you have, and void of detail. Since this practically begs to be broken down and analyzed, let's do it.

Although you know you are afraid to spar him, you want to ask a few broader questions to see if the fear goes further than that. When is it that you are afraid?

* Before class?
* When he is warming up?
* When the class is working on drills?
* When we are sparring?

You have decided that the first three are not a concern, and that you are keeping your original claim that it is when you spar with John that you feel the most apprehension. Let's break this general statement down by asking a few questions about it.

* Because John is an advanced student?
* Because he has poor control?
* Because I might look bad in front of the other students?
* Because I don't want to admit that I'm not as good as I think I am?

Let's say you are afraid of all of these things. Now you need to do is rate them as to the degree of fear they cause. Here is the order you decided on.

*You have absolutely convinced yourself that you will be
killed if you spar the big mean black belt!*

1. I'm afraid because John is an advanced student.
2. I'm afraid I will look bad in front of the class.
3. I'm afraid of his lack of control.
4. I'm afraid to find out I'm not as good as I thought.

Now you are going to examine each of these fears to determine to what degree they are a distortion of your imagination. Let's look at the third statement, one that could cause you some physical pain: I'm afraid of his lack of control.

Q.   Could his lack of control kill me?
A.   There may be a remote possibility, but he hasn't killed anyone else. Sure, he's landed some hard kicks and punches on people, but everyone has survived. I guess I'm O.K. that he is not going to kill me.
Q.   Could he cripple me for life?
A.   Sure, there is a remote possibility, but no one has ever been crippled by him. With all of the protective equipment I wear, the possibility is slim to none that it will happen.
Q.   Could he hurt me a little?
A.   Yes. He has hurt a few people, but getting kicked and punched is what the martial arts are all about. After all, I get whacked around in class to reduce the chance of my getting hurt seriously on the street.
Q.   Can I live with those hurts?
A.   Yes. I've been hurt before, and I survived and even learned from the experiences. Hey, I'm in a fighting class, not a quilting class.

When you break it down and see the reality of what can and might happen, the fear dissolves. No one wants to get seriously hurt or killed in their training, but the acceptance of bangs, bruises and sprains is necessary to progress in the fighting arts.

Now let's examine your first concern: John is an advanced student.

For our purposes, let's say you are a green belt with two years experience, and John is a black belt with ten years of training. Is his rank and experience the reason you to fear him? Once again, let's break it down.

Q. Am I afraid of his black cotton belt?

A. No. It's just cloth.

Q. Am I afraid of John?

A. Yes, his advanced punches and kicks can easily score on me.

Q. So what happens when he scores on you?

A. Nothing. He is a black belt; it's to be expected.

Q. Do his techniques hurt you?

A. Once in a while one lands extra hard.

Q. What do you do when that happens?

A. I just keep on sparring.

Q. Well, if you are not overly concerned about getting hit hard once in a while, and you have accepted the idea that he is a black belt and will probably score on you most of the time, what is your fear?

A. Uh . . .

Q. When he lands one, can you stop and ask him about it? Can you ask him how you should have defended yourself better?

A. Sure, he's very helpful.

Q. Would you learn something from what he tells you?

A. Now that I think about it, I guess I always learn something from him.

Q. So it doesn't bother you when he scores on you, you have accepted the occasional hard kick or punch when sparring with an advanced person, and you usually learn from him. Why then are you afraid of him?

A. Hmm. Maybe I'm not so afraid of him as I thought.

For you psychology buffs, this is called "cognitive restructuring" or "rational thinking." Asking yourself questions and answering them is one way to not only reduce or eliminate your imagined fear, but also to learn a little about yourself. Although I have shortened the process here due to space, you can stretch it out and break it down as far as you need to get control of your fear. The end result with John, is that you will be able to train with him in the future without your imagination causing you to freeze.

63

Desensitizing

Gordon Liddy, one of Richard Nixon's Watergate conspirators, wrote in his book, *Will*, that as a result of a childhood experience, he had a deathly fear, a manufactured one, of rats. Liddy is an individual who approaches problems with unique solutions. For this one, he conquered his fear through culinary means: He captured a large rat, killed it, cooked it a little over a small fire, and ate it.

Don't misread this and think that you have to eat the black belt who is causing you the grief. It's important, however, that you confront your manufactured fear and deal with it positively.

Let's use the same example as before that you are a green belt fearful of sparring with John, a black belt. You have yet to spar with him, but you are convinced that when you do, you will be painfully killed. But since you have been reading this chapter, you know that your fear is a manufactured one. It's not like he is going to leap out at you from a dark alley; he is just a concern, a worry in your mind that is causing you so much fear that it may ultimately hurt your martial arts progress. You need to face the situation head on; you need to set a goal of sparring with Big Bad John. You could do this by simply gritting your teeth and challenging him to a match, but that just might backfire if John perceives your demand as being disrespectful. A better approach is to work gradually toward your goal of reducing your fear. This will allow you to lay a sound foundation of confidence that will eventually support your sparring with him.

First, you are going to talk to him. If you haven't formally met him, take a moment before class to introduce yourself, and tell him you have admired his sparring ability for a long time. Tell him that you especially liked the way he fought in his last competition. You can accomplish a lot with honey, and nothing breaks the ice like a compliment. For sure, the next time you approach him, he will remember you.

Next time you talk, ask his advice on developing, say, a stronger reverse punch, since you are really impressed with the speed and power of his. Show him yours and ask what he suggests you could do to make yours better.

By approaching him and talking to him these first two times,

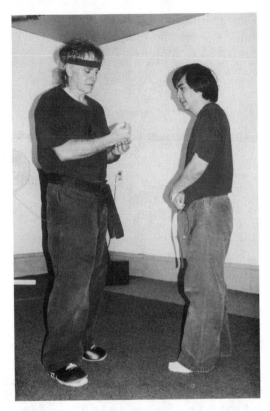

To begin reducing your fear, ask the source of your anxiety his advice on punching. Would a killer actually take the time to help you?

you have desensitized yourself to the monster that you have created in your mind. Think about it. Monsters don't smile, talk nicely and demonstrate their fighting methods. They just kill their prey. Since you haven't been killed, he must not be a monster. Therefore, he must be a nice guy who is willing to help you.

If this sounds simplistic, it's because it's supposed to be.

Next, you want to talk to him about his ideas concerning sparring. Ask how he uses his reverse punch to get inside an opponent's guard, or how he uses that awesome roundhouse kick when attacking, defending and faking. When he

When you feel the time is right, ask the source of your fear to spar. He may score on you, but your fear is dissolving.

demonstrates these things on you, you will have passed another barrier, that of being kicked and punched at by him, though in a controlled and limited fashion. And hey, you survived the experience.

When you feel you have laid a solid foundation of confidence (only you know when you have reached that point), ask John if the two of you could spar slowly. Don't make it a challenge, but ask if he would point out where you could improve. Unless he is an ego-driven jerk, he's not going to go into the session trying to rip you apart. Sure, he is going to score on you, but you are nonetheless surviving the moment, and your fear is quickly dissolving. By having approached the sparring session in gradual, confidence-building stages, you will have systematically chipped away all that your imagination had created. The end result is that you are now interacting with the very thing that you once feared.

The next to last stage is to spar fast. Because you have de-sensitized the fear, you only feel anxiety now, just a little ner-vousness. You might not even feel that. Once you start mixing it up, you might find the anticipated moment to be almost anti-climatic. Yes, he is scoring on you right and left, but after all, he is a senior student. He is not killing you; he's helping you learn. This is not the sort of thing that monsters do.

Lastly, you are going to do something that will act as a final cleansing to all of your manufactured fear. You are going to tell John about it. Tell him how you felt about him, how you practi-cally had a phobia about fighting him. But due to his kind help, you have dissolved that barrier that existed only in your mind. By saying this out loud to him, it's sort of a way of finalizing the defeat of the obstacle, and a way of imprinting your positive achievement in your mind.

Your courage to spar with John is not a demonstration that you lack fear, but rather an acceptance that in order to defeat unrealistic fear, you must look it straight in the eye. You must strip the falseness away, and use whatever anxieties that are left as energy. This is something you must do, because to remain in a state of manufactured fear is to not be in control of yourself or your growth in the martial arts.

Self-Hypnosis And Mental Imagery
Refer back to what you learned about using autosuggestion and mental imagery as an additional tool to help you overcome manufactured fear. Real fear can also be reduced by giving your-self suggestions to use the biochemical symptoms of fear as fuel to make you fight hard or to run fast.

A WISE MAN KNOWS HIS LIMITATIONS
Just because you have tapped into your fears and have de-veloped tools to control them, doesn't mean you are now free to wade into a situation that is beyond your capabilities. Ask your-self if staying to fight a six-foot-four inch logger, armed with a 36-inch long, whirling chainsaw is a reasonable thing for you to do. In this case, you know that your fear is not manufactured in your imagination but is based on truth, that this guy can hack

you to teeny weeny bits. Just because you know that the fear is not imagined doesn't mean that you shouldn't do a speedy about-face and run like the wind.

6

Ready to Fight

I want to talk about what you need to do to prepare yourself for a real fight, one in which your life is in jeopardy. I'm not talking about moving around your classroom, playing tag with ineffectual kicks and punches, but rather facing a guy who is bent on ending your life. He may be high on alcohol or drugs, mentally ill, enraged at something you did or thinks you did, or maybe he just wants to kill you for some reason that makes sense to him.

In my more than three decades in the martial arts, I have seen, met, and trained with fighters who have possessed extraordinary speed, power and fighting ability. I have trained with or attended seminars with such names as Chuck Norris, Joe Lewis, Wally Jay, Duke Moore, Tony Ho, Remy Presas and others. I have also been fortunate enough to see the late Bruce Lee and Ed Parker in person as they demonstrated their most incredible skills. There have been other experts who were just as incredible, though not famous since they had never sought the public eye. These are guys who have used their skills in the street; guys who have been there.

But just because you are a champion or just because you hold high rank and cool titles doesn't mean you have the mental fortitude to survive a life-and-death fight to the bloody end. I'm talking about fighting with all-out intensity and with

69

maximum spirit to do whatever it takes to beat an attacker into bloody submission. I'm talking about continuing to fight when that nauseatingly loud cracking sound you just heard was your forearm bone, continuing to fight though you are hacking blood from internal injuries and spitting out broken teeth chips. I'm talking about an all-out struggle for your life or the life of a loved one.

There are many stories around of otherwise excellent martial artists who were quickly beaten into the sidewalk by a tavern tough guy or an outlaw biker, people who have not been trained in karate or jujitsu, but have learned how to fight from experience on the street and in prison. They never learned to go easy on their partner, never heard of the concept of pulling their punches, or stopping a sparring session because their partner landed a blow too hard. What they have learned, however, is that in order to survive in the streets, they have to keep fighting no matter how much it hurts. Life on the mean streets has taught them a Pit Bull mentality– to never, ever give up.

I know one champion karate fighter who has earned so many trophies that if they were melted down he could build a dozen or more full-sized cars. He can pretty much put his fist or foot wherever he wants to and there isn't much his opponent can do about it. In addition to his incredible physical skill, he has another trait that is a rarity among champions, especially fighters like him who have graced the cover of martial arts magazines– honesty. He has told me more than once that he has doubts as to how well he would do in a real fight, a bloodletting, knock-down drag out. "I can play tournament tag," he says. "But if I had to fight for real, I don't know how I would do."

Here is a guy whose techniques are incredibly fast, awesomely powerful, and who can deliver them with the precise timing of a Swiss watch. Couple this physical ability with the right attitude, and my friend could be the terror of the streets if he chose to live that kind of lifestyle. But he doesn't have this attitude because he wasn't born with it, his growing-up environment didn't require it, and he has never made an effort to train for it.

There are many martial artists in this same boat. So how can you get a survivalist mind if you weren't born with it and have never had a need to acquire it? What else can you do short of getting into street fights with people who fight back with the intent of killing you?

Use Your Ol' Gray Matter

When in doubt as to what to do, return to that little dojo in your head– your brain. With a little effort, you can reach deep into it and pull out that rage that is simmering just below the surface. You don't have rage, you say? Oh yes you do, I reply. Even the most pacifistic, mellow couch potato is capable of extraordinary violence, and here is how you can test to see. Walk up to the pacifistic couch potato's five-year-old daughter, grab her by the back of her neck and begin to walk away with her. Over your shoulder, say something like, "Thanks a lot for your kid. I've been wanting one just like her." Now watch that pacifist turn into Rambo.

Everyone has something in their subconscious mind or perhaps right on the surface of their mind that when tapped can spark a ferocity that will intensify their ability to fight. What do you have festering in yours? Any of the following?

* An annoying mother-in-law
* An ex-spouse
* An overbearing coworker
* A rude and lousy waiter
* A boss who is both a dictator and stupid
* A harassing bill collector
* IRS
* That driver who cut you off
* The vandals who put graffiti on your house
* Your noisy neighbor

You probably have some of these (hopefully not all) simmering on a back burner in your brain, and maybe a few other issues of your own. What we are going to do now is bring one or two of those issues to the surface and blow them out the end of your fist and feet. Now, I've had people argue with me that punching and kicking your personal issues is not a healthy thing to do.

71

Well, its worked for me, and I've seen it work for other people, too. Many psychologists believe it's healthy, and some go so far as to suggest that people have a punching bag in their office. Others have even suggested that high-stress office workers occasionally duke it out with Nerf bats.

A city's police administration, mayor and citizens frown on over-stressed officers beating the dog doo-doo out of people. In my nearly three decades of police work, there were countless times I wanted to, but instead, I later took out my frustration in my school on the heavy bag, repping in the air, or on a sparring partner. I would reach deep into myself and pull out the rage, frustration and stress, and release it through my techniques. It not only made me feel a whole heck of a lot better, but it made my movements especially explosive.

One way to bring it out is with a drill called Red-Line, a concept Chuck Norris wrote about several years ago as a way to develop speed. It will definitely do that, but I've found that it's also a great drill to release those issues we have cooking in our brains. Here is how it's done.

Red-Line Drill

The drill consists of four sets of ten reps each, executed at medium speed, fast speed, red-line speed, and then fast speed again.

Medium Speed: Reps performed at this speed are executed at half the speed you consider fast, while emphasizing good form. Mentally, you will retrieve an issue you have festering, say, that jerk who nearly ran you into the guardrail on the freeway then laughed and flipped you an obscene gesture. Since striking back at him in a fit of road rage would get you in lots of trouble, you are going to trash the bozo in your mind as you attack the air.

Begin by visualizing the guy in front of you. Though you are only executing your moves at medium speed, do a front kick/ reverse punch combination with the same mental intensity you would use if you were going hard and fast. This might be a little difficult if you have not done this before, but it can be done. In fact, you can do it when moving much slower, even tai chi slow.

It's an excellent way to learn to bring intense emotion to the surface, but then control it by moving at a slow pace. Grimace as you execute your kick, tense your muscles when your foot hits the imaginary target, set it down, and launch your medium-speed backfist at the freeway creep's ear. Feel the force rush out of your body as it hits the target, then relax your arm and return it to the ready position. Exhale through your nose and contract your stomach muscles on each imagined impact.

Do one set of 10 reps on each side.

Fast Speed: Using the mental intensity you stirred up at medium speed, you are now going to launch that front kick and reverse punch as fast as you can while maintaining good form. Your fast blows are going to smash the imagined target with all the intensity you can muster. When you see that guy in front of you—his sneering lips, his bloodshot eyes, his unwashed appearance, his defiant jaw—you are going to want to smash him like a dropped watermelon.

Do one set of 10 reps on each side.

Red-Line Speed: OK, take a big breath because now you are going to go full bore, faster and harder than you have ever moved before. In my school we call Red-Line "going nuts." The set you did at Fast Speed was your fastest with good form. This time, however, you are going to be more concerned about moving faster and harder than about maintaining proper form. If you overextend your punching arm, so be it. If you lose your balance a little and have to shuffle your feet to catch yourself, oh well. Your primary emphasis is on moving like a madman.

See that freeway creep in front of you. He's taunting you now, he's talking about kidnapping your grandmother, about poisoning your dog, about running his house key down the side of your car. Do like many Hollywood actors do when they have to act out a scene in which they have to cry or show some other emotion. They recall a painful moment out of their lives, like a childhood memory of losing a kitten, and then build on that emotion, exaggerating and intensifying it until tears flow down their cheeks.

You can do the same. Maybe the freeway creep just perturbed you a little, but the more you stir that feeling, the bigger it becomes and the more emotion you are able to release from it. You want to create an intense motivation that will take you over the top, enabling you to move faster and hit harder than ever before.

I always start this set by taking a few fast, shallow breaths, almost as if I were trying to hyperventilate. I repetitiously splay my fingers and clench my fists as I feel the power and rage course through my arms, shoulders, chest, abdomen and legs. Sometimes I pace like a wild jungle cat in a zoo, wanting to leap through the steel bars and rip a tourist to shreds.

Do one set of 10 reps on each side.

Fast Speed: On this last set, you are going to return to fast speed again since your form was less than what it should be in Red-Line. Again, bring forth the mental image of the freeway creep and hit him as fast and hard as you can while still maintaining good form.

Do one set of 10 reps.

This is an exhausting drill, but when it's practiced two or three times a week, it will increase your speed and help you learn to release the necessary intensity to fight fiercely. Once you can bring it out easily in the Red-Line Drill, you will find that you can also bring it out when working the heavy bag, practicing drills with a training partner, sparring, and when doing your kata. Since you are purposely bringing out the intensity, you have control over it– it doesn't control you. Think of it as controlled rage.

When you tap on the issues simmering in your mind, you will be absolutely amazed at the change in your techniques. But you must continue to work at harnessing this controlled rage, or you will slip back into your old way of using only the speed and power of your muscles. Think of it this way. If you are already fast and powerful, think how much greater your speed and power will be when you incorporate your mind.

Let's now talk about a subject that may be unpleasant, but you must think about it if you are to have self-knowledge.

CAN YOU KILL?

The first day I strapped my pistol belt over my blue police uniform, I asked myself if I could really kill someone if the situation warranted it. I thought about what that experience would be like– the gut wrenching terror, the explosion of bullets, the screams, the distorted face of the person I shot, the heavy thump of his body hitting the floor– and decided that, no matter how horrific the experience, I could shoot and kill someone if my life or another's life was in grave danger. I hoped that I could get through my career without having to do it, but I knew that if it came down to my having to drop the hammer, I could.

I carried that thought with me every day of my 29 years in police work. No, I wasn't trigger-happy, I was just mentally prepared to do what is arguably the most serious thing one human can do to another. I felt it was important to be mentally prepared to kill, because when the situation calls for it in police work, there is seldom time to think consciously. The moment is usually an explosive one that happens in the blink of an eye, leaving little or no time to think. Any hesitation could cost me my life or someone else's. I wanted to always be mentally prepared so I would act without hesitation. Three years later I was in my first shooting, and my mental preparation paid off.

I also thought about whether I had the intestinal fortitude to kill someone with my bare hands. I certainly knew how to do it, but could I? It's one thing pulling a trigger when I'm several feet away from a threat, but it's much more personal to beat the life out of someone with my feet and hands. What if a bad guy disarmed me and I had to fight him hand-to-hand. Could I kill him to protect myself? I again answered yes.

I got in a lot of fights as a police officer, probably hundreds. While the thought of killing was not a conscious thought every time I struggled with a resistor, I was comfortable knowing that if the fight deteriorated and turned into a survival situation, I was mentally prepared to use deadly force with my hands.

Is this sort of thinking sick? No, it's smart. As a police officer, I was paid to protect the community, which meant that in an extreme situation, I might have to use deadly force. That's what I got the big bucks for. If I was unable to use that level of force

75

You need to ask yourself: "Could I complete this technique and take his life?"

and I was killed, or an innocent person was killed, what good was I as a protector?

During my career, I saw two or three rookie officers let it be known that they would never use deadly force, no matter what the situation. Somehow they had slipped through the psychological examination without their feelings being uncovered. But as soon as it was known, no other officers would work with them, and the rookies were quickly terminated.

As a martial artist, you train with techniques that can kill when executed under specific circumstances. Have you thought about whether you could take another person's life using your knowledge? If you are not in law enforcement, you have much more freedom to say that you won't or can't. If this is your answer, I'm not going to try to persuade you to change your value system, religion or whatever other reason you have. But I do want you to consider another question that I hope you give some serious thought to, because it's one that needs to be answered.

What are you going to do if you are in a situation that calls for deadly force? True, if you are not in law enforcement the chance of your being exposed to this dilemma is slim, but it can still happen– someone attacks you with a deadly weapon, someone breaks into your home and grabs your spouse or child, you walk into the middle of someone being stabbed (which I have), or any number of other situations that take place every day in this country. You need to consider what you would do in lieu of using deadly force if your restraint holds don't do the job, your clever verbiage is ineffectual, or any other thing you can think of doesn't work for you.

I hope this never becomes an issue for you.

The Mental Edge

Edge

~Revised

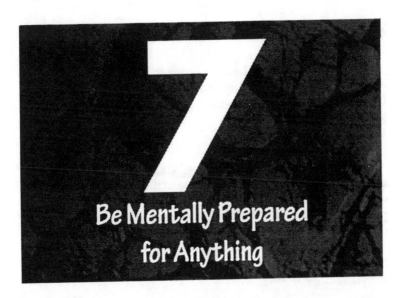

7

Be Mentally Prepared
for Anything

Although many people are afraid of that shadowy figure who steps out of the dark and rushes at you with a razor-sharp sickle, the reality is that such surprise occurrences seldom happen. Ninety-nine times out of 100, there was some indication of a threat, but the victims either didn't perceive it, or didn't believe it even though they got a hint of something not quite right. Indeed, most victims of assault were in what I call the White Zone, a place where they couldn't see a blimp if it landed on their heads.

ZONES OF MENTAL AWARENESS

There are four zones of mental awareness. To make it easy for our discussion, let's color-code them: White, Yellow, Orange and Red. These mental stages go from total unawareness to complete involvement in a situation. While most people fluctuate from one zone to another as the situation dictates, far too many people will fail to make the move because they are unaware and don't see a reason for it. I would like to think that martial artists would be more aware of their environment than other folks, but this isn't true. Those students who are just into the social aspects of the school, sport fighting, or only want a unique way to get into shape, are more likely not to think in terms of street survival, at least no more so than the average non-martial artist. This is a dangerous and potentially fatal error.

Let's take a look at the four zones to see how you can use them to ensure you get through your day in one piece in this increasingly crazy world. Let's begin with that potentially fatal place called The White Zone.

The White Zone

People who walk around in the White Zone make excellent crime victims because their heads are in the clouds. They are the ones whose noses are buried in books as they ride on public transportation, walk along the streets bobbing to headphone music, doze in their cars as they wait for their spouse, lose themselves in a window display, walk obliviously past a group of gang members, and leave their cars running as they run into convenience stores.

Dozing in the White Zone is a dangerous place to be.

I occasionally ride a train into town. There are always a handful of people reading their paperbacks, knitting, dozing or staring trance-like out the windows. They never look up as a half dozen gang members bebop aboard, flashing their gang signs, and insulting riders. They are oblivious to drunk transients stumbling into people, and they haven't a clue that there are beady eyes looking at their handbags or attache cases.

Think of the White Zone as a place that leaves the door wide open to attack.

The Yellow Zone

As a martial artist who thinks about street defense (hopefully, you do), you will have a heightened sense of mental awareness. Even when you are not in danger, your brain will be in a state of relaxed alertness, perceptive to the potential hazards around you. As you walk to your car in a parking lot, you are aware of all the places where a threat could be hiding. You make note of the van and the large tree that block your view, the dumpster where you have seen transients loitering in the past, and the darkened alleyway where you have noticed scruffy characters walking in and out.

Because of your training and your knowledge of crime in your town and neighborhood, you are aware of everything to your front, rear and sides. You have a sense of what is the norm, and when you perceive something that isn't part of it, you watch it until it's OK in your mind. Although the statistics are in your favor that you are not going to get jumped, you know that there is always that possibility, and this is where alertnesss counts.

Heightened mental awareness is what the Yellow Zone is all about.

The Orange Zone

Things are getting a little froggy (a police expression for suspicious) in this zone. But since you were going about your day in the Yellow Zone, you quickly perceive something suspicious, and your brain begins putting a plan into action. Here are a couple of examples.

You are at your favorite pub having a brew with a buddy, and you have noticed a couple of big, drunk guys playing a noisy

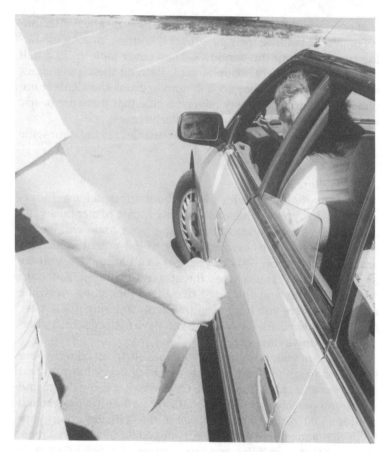

Because you are alert in the Yellow Zone, you can see the approaching threat in the side mirror.

game of pool. Later when you get up to use the restroom, one of the drunks steps in your path and gives you an Elvis-Presley-lip snarl.

You and your girl friend are walking to your car, and as you round the corner, you see someone's butt sticking out of your passenger door.

You instantly perceive danger in both these situations because you are in a heightened state of mental awareness. If you had been mentally dozing in the White Zone, you wouldn't have noticed the drunk pool players earlier, and you wouldn't have seen the danger in your car until you were standing next to it. Then when you did realize there was danger, if indeed you did, you would be startled with surprise and you might even freeze. It's a long trip for your mind to go from the White Zone to the Orange Zone.

It's an even longer trip when you have to go to the Red Zone.

My awareness allows me to defend myself using the car door.

The Red Zone

You're smack in it now; it's hit the fan. The drunk in the bar swings the pool stick; the guy prowling your car turns toward you and advances with a tire iron. From the Orange Zone, you are ready and your reaction is instantaneous. If you had been in the White Zone, you still wouldn't have a clue of the danger about to befall you. Even if you suddenly became aware, the Red Zone is a long ways to go from obliviousness. That pool stick will get you first, and so will the tire iron.

Stay mentally alert and be ready for anything. Stay in the Yellow Zone.

IS THERE A SIXTH SENSE?

Bruce Lee argued that there is no sixth sense, but rather a heightened awareness from the five senses. Some call this a "gut feeling" or "intuition," others get mystical and say they have extrasensory perception. By whatever name it's called, it's a powerful feeling based on your life experiences that you should heed because it warns you about people, places and things. And since you are continuously adding to your sixth sense through your daily experiences, you are right now at your very best.

The problem is that too often we dismiss these feelings as stupid or meaningless. But they aren't. They are based on something, and you must heed them until you know for sure that that something is OK.

I'm going to brag for a second to make a point. As I've mentioned a few times in this book, I spent 29 years in police work and experienced more resist arrest situations in the form of scuffles and all-out brawls than I could ever count. But only once was I struck, a time when I happened to be in the path of a board swung by an angry neighbor at another neighbor.

I always relied on my sixth sense. If I felt that a guy was going to go hard, I jumped in first and applied a technique before he had the opportunity. If I had a feeling about a group of people or a place I was approaching, I always did so with great caution and with correct technique. I was able to do this because I was never in the White Zone, and always relied on my so-called sixth sense.

Many victims I have interviewed, talked about the danger signals they missed or ignored before they became a crime statistic. "I can see now that I shouldn't have just walked into that bar when I saw all those outlaw motorcycles parked outside." Later, when they were filing a report with me at the hospital, they realized the importance of those signs they had unfortunately ignored.

Don't you ignore them. To be a complete martial artist, a warrior, you must be mentally aware and you must listen to your sixth sense. It doesn't just kick in when you walk into your martial arts school and then shut off when you walk out the door after training. Let me say it again: You must be in the Yellow Zone at all times.

I used to tell students that the only time they can be in the White Zone is when relaxing in their homes. But after investigating cases of home intrusion robberies by gun-wielding gang members, burglaries where the crooks came in when the occupants were sleeping in bed, and rapes where the suspects smashed through a door to get to their victim, I'm no longer so sure that's good advice. You be the judge of your own situation.

The Mental Edge
~Revised

8

Be the Best You Can Be

Obstacles Are Those Frightful
Things You See When You
Take Your Eyes Off Your Goal
Henry Ford

There are generally two reasons people begin training in martial arts: to beat the crap out of the school bully or to develop enough confidence in this sometimes scary world to walk down the street knowing they have an advantage to protect themselves and their loved ones. If either of these reasons are yours, you no doubt see the fighting arts as just fighting. But as time passes and you build a solid base of knowledge, you discover that studying the martial arts is much more than just fighting others. It's also about facing yourself, that tough, ever-present opponent who usually gives you the biggest fight of all. Let's call him The Destroyer, because that is what he is– but only if he wins.

FIGHTING THE DESTROYER

If you have trained for a couple of years, you have no doubt discovered this tough opponent. If you are just getting into the arts, trust me, you will. He's the one who was with you during that first class when you felt silly learning the bow, and he was the one who made you awkward and self-conscious those first few lessons. You can't get away from this person; he's like your shadow. But he will lay low from time to time, and you should consider those good times because that is when you will make the most progress. Don't relax, though, because it's a guarantee he will be back, right there in your face testing your will and fortitude.

Let's examine ways to combat this opponent so you can continue to progress on your path to being the best you can be. Keep in mind that he is not going to be a one-time fight, but rather a sporadic one that will be always be a thorn in your paw.

I began my training in the summer of 1965. I trained hard and by the following summer I had developed enough skill that I was able to defend myself in a couple of street encounters. So why have I continued to train to this day? Why have I continued to put myself through the pain, sweat, and injuries of intense workouts, when I could defend myself pretty well after just a year of training? The answer lies in a personal goal that I established early on: While I've never cared if I'm better than the next guy, or worse, I've always wanted to be the best that I could be.

Fortunately, I knew of The Destroyer's existence early in my martial arts career, as he had already showed himself during the six years I had been weight training. I knew The Destroyer for what he was and realized that to be the best I could be, I had to continually fight all the human frailties, such as fear, laziness, and self-satisfaction that make up his personality. The fight is still going on because he never goes away.

Although I have been fighting this guy for a long time, it has been worth every minute of the struggle. I know that every time I "score a point" on The Destroyer, I grow as a person and as a martial artist.

This chapter examines The Destroyer and a few of the challenges he tosses at you as you strive to be the best you can be. The challenges discussed here are typical of the many that you will discover on your bumpy path to physical skill and self-discovery. They become unsurmountable only when you allow them to weaken your resolve to fight.

If you see yourself in some of the following sections, know that it's never too late to change. Take action immediately and meet the challenge head on. Never sit in one place and tell yourself you are defeated, because you lose only when you do nothing.

So, put on your sparring equipment because it's time to get on your way to being the best you can be.

THE TRAINING HABIT

Skipping class or your solo workout is as easy as pie to do. You skip one workout and that lazy part of your brain wakes up just long enough to say, "Hey, cool. That was so easy I think I'll do that again." So you skip another workout, and another, and soon you are skipping one or two a week. Before you realize it, you form a habit. By skipping a series of workouts, you establish a pattern, an automatic response to your slightest hesitation not to train. You begin filling training time with other activities, and you convince yourself that it's next to impossible to get back into the training habit.

To be the best you can be, you absolutely need to rid yourself of negative habits and replace them with positive ones. You must firmly implant in your mind that missed workouts will do nothing for your progress and is time lost on your path to martial arts skill and knowledge. You should feel a sense of guilt about missed classes, because valuable time has passed and is lost forever.

Think of it this way. You are only given so much time on Earth and if you have chosen to make the martial arts part of your life, and you are working toward a specific goal, then allotting time to train is part of the deal. But if you replace that time with, say, TV watching, or going to a party, you have weakened your discipline and cheated your goal, your art, and yourself.

My Personal Schedule

What I've found helpful over the years is my habit of doing something toward my art every day. No, I don't do punches and kicks every day, nor do I recommend that you do. Your body needs to rest. But I've programmed myself to do something each day so that my mind stays disciplined and my goal of continual improvement stays alive.

I've followed many different schedules over the years (variety is important); my current one is as follows.

One way to develop a training habit is work out with a friend and then push each other to do better.

Mon: Martial Arts (M.A.) class - 2 Hrs.	Weights - neck
Tues: M.A. - read or write or view videos	Weights - shoulders, biceps
Wed: M.A. - class - 2 Hrs.	Weights - forearms
Thurs: M.A. - read or write or view videos	Weights: triceps
Fri: M.A. - read or write or view videos	Weights: back
Sat: M.A. - light workout	No weight workout
Sun: M.A. - read or write or view video	Weights: Chest

On Monday and Wednesday, I teach and train in my school. On Tuesday, Thursday and Saturday, I have a choice of reading or writing, depending on what I think I need or what will spark my interest that day. For example, if I'm working on a martial arts magazine article or book, I'll write. If I just want to relax, I'll read something on the fighting arts or look at one of my many tapes. Sometimes I'll call my instructor and chat. If I have an abundance of energy on Saturday, I'll solo train, or workout with my wife or daughter.

I work one body part a day with the weights, having discovered that hitting a muscle group once every seven days is all I need. Some people may think this is not enough, but I make progress and have energy to burn. You have to find what works for you.

Although my class time is rigid, the other days aren't. I'm a full-time writer, so if I'm working on a martial arts writing project, I'll write for about three hours a day, which takes care of the day's requirement. But if I'm working on a non-martial arts writing job, I'll read a martial arts magazine or book, or slip a video into my office VCR for a few minutes.

My mind has accepted this pattern and it has become an entrenched habit– one that I feel is positive. Some might judge it to be fanatical, but a close examination of the times shows there are lots of hours left for other things. Although I may have committed myself to do something in the martial arts every day, there is still plenty of time for family, friends, movies and other interests. For example, if I thumb through a martial arts magazine for 15 minutes on Tuesday, I still have 23 hours and 45 minutes to do other things. Even my two-hour class day leaves me with 22 hours for other things.

91

I have become so ingrained with this habit, that on those rare days when some unexpected event prevents me from doing something toward my art, I have a deep feeling of having lost something valuable to me. It's like I skipped a meal and I'm hungry.

You have to develop your own schedule, one that is habit forming. Don't say that there isn't enough time in the day for you to do something toward your art; that is absolute nonsense. You can read on the toilet (you do have time for the toilet, don't you?), in the bathtub, before you go to sleep at night, or before you get up in the morning. You can stretch while watching TV, or throw kicks at the screen, or thumb through this book. There are zillions of moments throughout your day when you can slip in a little time for the martial arts. You just have to be honest with yourself and find them. When you do, your mind will quickly condition itself to the schedule, and you will be surprised how easy it is not to skip any part of it.

DON'T SETTLE IN THE COMFORT ZONE

We all know an armchair athlete. He is the guy who slumps deeply into his favorite chair and watches the game on television. His beer is cold and his team is winning. This guy has entered a place far worse than the Twilight Zone. He has just slipped into that nearly inescapable place called, The Comfort Zone.

Maybe the name of the place doesn't sound so terrible, but be on guard because it's a dangerous, seductive place where The Destroyer loves to hang out. It's so comfy that you will have trouble getting out of that chair, away from the television, never again to be a participant. The status quo is an easy place to be. But it takes work to push onward and upward, because your natural tendency is to seek out and bask in what is the easiest and most comfortable.

If you *really* need to rest, then treat yourself to some relaxation and extra sleep. But be careful! It's easy to get fooled and convince yourself to skip a workout, since it's much easier to kick back and not get sweaty, tired and bruised.

Because you have made a decision to see how far you can go physically and mentally in the fighting arts, you need to pull yourself out of your comfort zone and back into a positive routine of training. But how do you get your mind to make the switch? It's actually easy once you start seeing the results you get from it. When you go to class regularly, you learn new techniques, improve old ones, strengthen your body, develop your reflexes, and enhance all the mental skills that are involved in your art. In other words: You make progress. On the other hand, when you stay in your comfort zone, you don't progress at all. In fact, you begin to slowly regress– ßthen quickly regress.

Sometimes Discipline Can Be Lonely

It can be grueling to put in the extra training time required for competition, belt advancement, or getting back into shape after an illness. During my competitive years, there were many times, especially during those final weeks before a tournament, when I wanted to just read a novel or go to a movie instead of facing another exhausting workout. That lazy part of me was always there, hovering just over my shoulder, offering me all the riches of the sofa, potato chips and a soda. The Destroyer's voice was sweet and sensual: "You know your kata already, besides, what do you need with another trophy? Take it easy, dude. Just relax and get comfy."

I must admit that there were times when the voice was powerfully seductive, even convincing, but I'm proud to say that I never yielded to it. Never once. I always convinced myself that competing at my very best was what I wanted to do. I wanted to compete better than I did the time before; I wanted to progress, not maintain what I had already achieved. I knew that it could be terribly lonely out there in the middle of the kata ring where the audience and judges were seeing the product of my preparation, all the effort I put into reaching that moment in time. They didn't care how much training I had avoided or how many movies I had seen. They were interested only in my skill.

It wasn't just competition that has kept me training over the years. As I write this, I have been training for 34 years, but I competed only for five of them. It was my career choice that kept me training more than the competition. I was in law enforcement first as a military policeman in Vietnam then as a police officer in Portland, Oregon, where I worked skid row, street gangs, dignitary protection, and some of the toughest areas Portland has to offer. My skill at handling myself was important to my survival. Trust me, there were times when it got real lonely on a back street late at night when it was just me and some doped up, inhuman psycho who wanted to rip off my head and stuff my shiny badge into the bloody meat. He didn't care about my skipped training. He was just concerned about how good I was at the moment, that is, whether I could hurt him and take away his freedom. With that thought paramount in my mind, I never missed a workout.

You Have To Decide

It's up to you. Are you going to be an armchair martial artist and settle into that comfort zone where life is easy because everything is just holding in place? Or are you going to be a fighter who puts in the extra effort, that extra bit of intestinal fortitude that will eventually pay off and pay off well?

It's your decision.

ARE YOU THAT GOOD?

Over the years, I've been asked by friends who don't know a side kick from a french fry, why I train so hard. Now that I'm over 50, they ask why I train at all (not surprisingly, those asking are void of muscle and ample of waistline). "You have been training since you were 19-years-old," they say, "and you have multiple black belts in karate, jujitsu and arnis. You have a room full of trophies and you were ranked in "Karate Illustrated" magazine as a Top Ten Karate competitor. Why do you keep training so hard?"

The answer is simple: I'm not that good, and I've always thought I could be better.

What about you? Are you so good that you can now kick back and take it easy? Sure, you're pretty good, maybe even real good. But wouldn't you like to be great?

To be the best you can be, you can't settle for just being good. If you're not careful, "being good" can easily turn into a Comfort Zone, a place where you settle in. Don't let it happen to you. You want to be the best you are capable of. You have an itch to scratch, a hunger to feed. You have got to keep on pushing and pushing and pushing and . . .

EXTRA EFFORT

Belt ranking in my school progresses like this: white, yellow, blue, blue second class, green, green second class, brown, brown second class, and black belt. On an average, green belt takes about one and a half to two years to earn. Although green belt is about half-way through the belt system, time wise it's actually about one third of the way to the coveted black belt, since the remaining succession of belts takes longer to earn.

An average student can reach green belt by attending class two or three times a week, while the above average student can possibly make it by attending only twice a week. At the green belt level, the student will have acquired fast and powerful karate basics and a good working knowledge of jujitsu and arnis. It's a level where the foundation is strong and where complex skills begin to show themselves.

In most schools, this middle point, whether it's symbolized by a green belt or some other color, is where a large percentage of students drop out. It's usually a point of growth stagnation, a plateau where only extra effort will once again get the student progressing. But if he isn't willing to put in the extra effort or doesn't yet realize that his old training regimen will no longer suffice, he will become discouraged, and that's where many people simply give up.

To achieve your very best, you must be willing to put in the extra effort to get there. Perhaps you have reached green belt or have reached a half way point to some other goal. It's important that you feel good about your accomplishment because few people make it that far. But now you need to stir up your hunger in order to see how much further you can go.

Talk To Your Instructor

Begin by talking to your instructor as to what you need to do to get your motivation in gear. He has an insight into what you need and hopefully knows you well enough to understand what motivates you. On the other hand, if you have been with him for a couple of years and he doesn't know what it takes to get you going, you should consider changing schools. If he is that much in the dark and doesn't care enough about his students to take the time to know them, then that could very well be the reason you are struggling with motivation.

Train With Higher Ranked Students

Train with a higher ranked friend or ask your instructor if you can train a few times with, say, the brown belt class. This will not only benefit you physically, but will tease you mentally by making you hungry to get the skill that goes with the advanced rank.

Use Your Creative Skills

Use your knowledge to develop new exercises, drills and fighting techniques. At this point in your training, you have acquired a large amount of knowledge upon which to draw from. In fact, you know much more than you think you do. For example, if you know 50 techniques, you actually know thousands when you start combining them into combinations and adding various types of footwork.

Consider a combination like the lead hand backfist followed by a rear hand straight punch. You can do it with your right side forward and with your left side forward. You can do it with an assortment of steps, leaps, and spins, moving forward, backwards, diagonally forward or backwards, and sideways. You can do it while down on one knee, both knees and even sitting on your butt. You can do it in your car, the shower, outside in the rain, or standing on a tree stump in a forest. When you run out of ideas, reverse the order and do the punch first, then the backfist, practicing the same variety of drills you did with backfist and punch. When you tire of those, you can lead the combination with a kick, and when you get tired of that, you can follow the combination with a kick.

Hey, if you came up with all that with just two techniques, think about the possibilities with all the others you know. Start combining techniques and get creative as to the many ways you can do them. This will not only spark your interest, but you will

longer have to train because you have reached the top (have you noticed how many "masters" teach but never train?), you are likely to be disappointed when you find those hard-earned skills fading. Do you think you will keep them forever without training any more? No way! In fact, you will very soon find that you can no longer do even the basics, and that's called REGRESSION, something that should be considered a bad, bad word.

To be the best you can be, you can't relax after reaching one goal or even ten goals. Striving to be the best means you are ever reaching and never satisfied with past achievements. Yes, you should pause to celebrate a goal reached or a job well done, but then you must resume moving upward. This is the time to take advantage of your forward momentum, and use its energy to keep you enthused and hungry for more.

How Goal Setting Made For A Comeback Story

I tell my personal comeback story here not because I want to hear myself tell it again (well OK, that's part of the reason), but because I want you to think in terms of never giving up, no matter what befalls you and no matter what you are told.

In 1983, I decided to enter an upcoming kata competition after staying away from karate tournaments for eight years. Eight years earlier, I had broken my knee cap and injured the tendons and muscles around my knee so severely that my doctors told me that I would have to retire from police work, walk with a cane the rest of my life, and definitely never practice martial arts again. Well, I didn't accept this decree. I fought hard to get my knee back in shape, enough so to toss away the cane (nine months later), return to my police duties (10 months later), and resume my martial arts training (three years later).

When I made the decision to enter the tournament, I knew there were three strikes against me: I was 37 years old, my knee would never be 100 percent, and I hadn't competed for several years. These were monstrous obstacles to overcome, and I was brooding about this when it dawned on me that my negative thinking was detrimental to what I wanted to do. Hey, I had defied the doctor's decree and had attained a level of success that a few years earlier looked impossible. So why was I letting these obstacles get to me? I needed a plan of action to get back into tournament competition.

The first part of my plan was to increase my training intensity so as to bring my skill to a level where I wouldn't embarrass myself in front of hundreds of people. I had been practicing my katas regularly, but black belt competition requires long, hard preparation, much more than regular training. No matter; I was hungry and mentally prepared to do whatever it took.

So I trained arduously, and within three months my katas were ready for show-time, though my knee was swollen and killing me. But I was feeling good because I had reached the first step of my goal. Now I was ready for the next one– competition.

The day of the tournament, I was filled with dread and excitement as I warmed up along the sidelines. The butterflies were having a riot in my stomach, and a little voice in my skull was asking repeatedly, "Why are you doing this?" Probably first time bungee jumpers ask themselves the same question before they take that hairy plunge. But I was there, committed and way too nervous to get philosophical.

Out of 20 competitors, I took fourth place. It was a tough competition, and I had to play off a tie to win the 12-inch high, red and gold trophy. I felt good about that win, and to this day it has a special place in my den where it sits proudly, representing my win over fear, age and physical limitations.

I took a few days to enjoy my accomplishment. I thought about retiring from competition, but I wondered if my comeback win had just

Sometimes small trophies mean more than big ones.

been a fluke. So I set another goal of competing to see if I was really a winning competitor.

At the next tournament I won second place, the one after that I nabbed a third, and at one of the biggest tournaments in the Northwest, I captured a first place win. I felt good about how far I had come, and once again I thought about retiring. I felt I had nothing more to prove to myself or anyone else.

A couple months passed, and once again I felt that familiar hunger, that itch to set some new goals. This time I set out to get rated in "Karate Illustrated" magazine's "Region 1, Top Ten Kata Competitor." This meant I had to get hungry to train hard, compete frequently, and win frequently in order to accumulate the required points to get rated over all the other competitors trying to do the same thing.

It was my hunger that provided me with the necessary energy to put in the extra training and to compete tournament after tournament. I kept at it, and by my 39th birthday my name appeared in the ratings. I was thrilled over this accomplishment because with a powerful mind set, I had successfully conquered many obstacles, especially the ol' knee injury.

I went on to win over 50 trophies and a few grand championships. But then in 1983 I blew my shoulder out while arresting a violent man on a skid row street, which brought my competition days to a painful halt. By the time my injury had recuperated to the point where I could have competed, I was no longer interested. I had moved on to other goals and objectives, which included increasing my rank in karate and jujitsu, and writing books.

What I learned from all this was that all those bumps in my path are just that, bumps. They are not insurmountable walls and they are not bottomless traps. They are challenges to meet and defeat. I know now that if I lose my legs, I'll scoot around on my hands and tackle my opponents. If I lose my arms, I'll be the best darn little head butter I can be.

SACRIFICING

We are a spoiled society. We want our drive-up meal in two minutes, we watch major motion pictures via our VCR in the comforts of our living room, we fly anywhere in the world in a matter of hours, and with a rectangular piece of plastic we buy virtually anything we want. And we can get all of these things quickly and easily.

Except skill in the martial arts.

Of course, there are rip-off schools that understand that we are the McDonalds' generation who want things now, so they offer contracts to students that promises a black belt after only 18 months (I recently heard of one that gives out black belts after six months of training). These schools are shams, fakes. Any school that awards a black belt in less than three years (it takes five years in my school) is giving out false confidence along with a meaningless belt.

Skill is something you acquire only after you recognize that you can't get it at a drive-up window or with a credit card. Real skill costs much more than just your monthly dues: it's something that costs you millions in blood, sweat, tears and sacrifice.

Those Who Train Alone

I'm a firm believer in practicing alone, in fact I wrote a book on it titled, *The Way Alone* that is available from Paladin Press. I encourage my students, actually I nag them relentlessly, to practice one or two days a week on their own. Some do and some don't, and I can tell in one glance who does because they look better than those who don't.

What is interesting, though not surprising, is that those students who always train one or two extra days on their own are my best students. They seldom miss class because they never yield to the temptations of sprawling on the sofa or having a brew after work with their buddies. They have committed themselves to their martial arts training. Their willingness to make personal sacrifices and to religiously put in extra training makes them better and moves them to the head of the class.

Fighting The Temptations

It is not always easy to say no to the many temptations that arise. At times, having a couple of beers with buddies at times can be much more inviting than an hour of getting punched and kicked. But when you have a powerful goal, you have strength to fight such temptations. When you put the devices discussed in this book into action– self-hypnosis, positive imagery, goal setting– your mind and heart will be determined. When you are confronted by all the delights of instant pleasure, you will see them for what they are and not let them interfere with your martial arts.

After a while, you won't see this as sacrificing. Pleasures you thought were going to be hard to give up, will no longer be so important, because your goal of being the best you can be will far overshadow these momentary pleasures.

WHY ME?

While training to be your best, you will be presented with some of life's cruel little jokes. It seems like every time you get ahead, you run headlong into an obstacle. It's like we used to say in the army when climbing a muddy hill, "Every time you take a step forward, you slide back two." Or as one of my advanced students lamented recently, "Whenever I decide to concentrate on improving my sparring and begin to see improvement, I jam a finger or sprain a toe. It never, ever fails."

The Rocky Path

The course of study you undertake in the martial arts is often referred to as "The Way," or "The Path." You no doubt have discovered that it's a rocky path, and some of the rocks are huge boulders. And there are pits, too, and alligators. If you are new in the arts and haven't seen this yet, understand that I'm not trying to deter you, I just want you to be prepared for your journey. To be your best, you need to know that there are going to be obstacles there waiting for you, and you need to be ready and willing to kick their butts.

I think it's ridiculous when a student jams a finger and stays home until the injury completely heals. What a waste of time! When eventually he does return– some never do because they slip into the habit of NOT training– he will be out of shape and will have fallen behind in class. What the heck would this person do if he jammed his finger in a real fight? Will he ask his assailant to wait a few days until it heals? Of course not. He would keep on fighting, and "keep on" is exactly how he should train.

That Which Does Not Kill You Makes You Stronger

I never view a sprained finger or any injury as a setback. Sure, I'm disappointed, but I immediately set on a training course in such a way, that I come away from my injury stronger in some other area. For example, I'll hold my injured hand behind me or hook it into my belt, and then work on drills and sparring using my remaining weapons. If it's a toe I've hurt, I'll work primarily on my hand techniques and do lots of leg stretching to keep my kicks flexible. Since I can't kick for a couple weeks, I can double the amount of time I usually spend on flexibility exercises. As a result, I always recuperate from my injuries a little stronger than before.

Save the self-pitying "Why Me?" to Olympic ice skater Nancy Kerrigan. You are a martial artist, a fighter, and your energy should be spent making these inevitable injuries a positive time, a time to make you stronger in another area. To be the best you can be, you must accept that there will be obstacles along your path, and that they will present themselves at the most inopportune times. But with acceptance of their lurking existence, and a positive outlook, you will be able to face them, defeat them, and grow stronger from the experience.

DON'T THINK SO MUCH

When you are too analytical of each phase of a technique, you risk missing the entire movement. I have found that students who think analytically at the wrong moment are hard to teach and have a hard time learning. As a teacher, this is frustrating because I know the student can do it, but his over-analytical mind is getting in his way.

Professor Remy Presas, founder of the martial art of Modern Arnis, teaches a 12-count striking and blocking drill with 24-inch rattan sticks. There are 12 offensive strikes to 12 vulnerable targets ranging from the top of the head to the ankle. The drill can be performed so that each strike flows smoothly into the next strike.

Back in the early '80s, when I first began teaching the drill, I broke each movement down into precise directions of force, footwork patterns, body angling and snapping of the wrist. I quickly discovered that this rather simple drill took several classes to teach because of what I thought was the students' confusion over the complexity of the movements. Actually, when I looked closer at what was going on, I realized that the students were confused because of how I was teaching the drill.

Since my approach wasn't working, I decided to experiment and teach it differently to a small group of new students. Actually, it wasn't a new way at all, but rather the way in which I was initially taught by Professor Presas. His way was to stand before the class and slowly proceed through the seemingly complicated weave of attack lines without explanation as to what he was doing and what the strikes represented. Later, he broke the individual movements down and explained what they were.

So, I led my students through the 12 strikes without explanation. There was some confusion at first because they wanted to analyze the movements, but instead of answering their questions, I demonstrated the pattern again. By the third time through, they realized I wasn't answering them or giving them time to analyze the movements. They could only follow. On the fourth time through, they were following me pretty well, and by the tenth time, they were emulating my arm, body and foot movements.

It was only then that I spent about 15 minutes giving an explanation about body positioning, footwork, flowing and so on. By the end of the class, the students not only could do the striking drill, but they had a good understanding of all the mechanics involved. They had achieved in less than 25 minutes, what had taken me three class periods to teach using my old method. They had learned because I had forced them to unclutter their minds and just do it.

I had learned something too— how to teach.

Children's lack of focus and inevitable horseplay can make them a real challenge to teach, but I find that their incredible ability to learn fast makes it worthwhile. They learn faster than adults because they don't analyze the material or try to put new information into familiar categories. Instead, children just emulate what they are taught.

There are times when you need to shut off your analytical mind and simply learn like children do.

There are times you should stop being so analytical and try to learn like a child.

WORDS

This is one of my favorite mind games, especially when training by myself. I think of it as role playing and a way of interpreting a specific feeling.

Concentration is important in the martial arts. If you are going up for the grand championship at the biggest tournament of the year, you can't be thinking of your grandmother's apple pie. Preparing to break a huge block of ice is not the time to be thinking about buying a new puppy. Concentration is paramount in the fighting arts, but it doesn't have to be difficult or boring.

"Words" is a fun and effective exercise to get your mind connected with your movements. There is no chanting or incense burning, but you do need a good imagination and a little ability to act. For example, when I practice a kata, I like to interpret the word "samurai." I've walked in the mountains of Japan and seen a zillion samurai movies, so the word has a definite connotation to me. To bring it out and translate it into my moves, I charge myself with a feeling of old Japan, and imagine that I'm a samurai in defense of an ancient mountain village at the foot of Mt. Fuji. Weird? Maybe, but it works for me.

Here is how you can do it. Simply choose a descriptive word that means something to you. Say you are working on a combination and have chosen the word "soft," which to you connotes a feeling of light, gentle, flowing movement. Your arms float in the air as if they were stalks of wheat riding on a summer breeze. Your kicks lift and settle back to the floor as light as a feather and without sound. Think of your techniques as so soft that if someone were to touch your wrist in mid-punch, your fist would be thrown off course.

Think of the word, "explosive" before you spar or shadow-box, then define the word with dynamite-like blasts ripping through your opponent's defenses.

Choose words that present an immediate and colorful picture in your mind. Here are a few good ones.

* Heavy	* Smooth	* Explosive
* Snappy	* Violent	* Enraged
* Floating	* Sharp	* Slicing

107

It is not important that you and your training partner agree on the connotations of the words, but it is important that you have a clear understanding of them, and can translate your feeling into your movements. As you progress, you may want to add new words to your list, or you may want to delete words that just aren't working for you.

This is one method of concentration that is made easy because it's fun. You will be totally involved mentally with your physical actions, because through your translation of the word, your mind and body will be working together, which is what concentration is all about.

PRACTICE HUMILITY

Do you have a guy in your class who struts, brags and acts like he invented the martial arts? He always has all the answers and never hesitates to show off, usually against lower belts. His mouth is never shut as he goes on and on about his exploits, his great wins in tournaments, and in every other area of his life. Unfortunately, there is always one of these guys around.

Let's say you are the guy.

It takes a lot of energy to be a braggart and to always be "on," always making sure that everyone knows how cool you are. It drains energy and it dilutes any good feelings you have from your accomplishments. The reality is that in spite of all your efforts, people really don't think you are cool; they hate what you are doing and avoid you like the plague.

Do you know someone, especially someone in the martial arts, who has a quiet inner confidence and never says a word about what he has done? People are usually attracted to this kind of personality. They like others who don't brag about themselves are capable of great deeds. And a humble person is especially loved when he offers help from a place deep in his heart, rather than from a place of ego.

The next time you accomplish something really big in your life, like earning your black belt, or walking away from a tournament with three big trophies, don't tell anyone, not one single person. It's hard to do, but when you refrain from tooting your own horn, you will feel something that you don't feel when you brag yourself up. It's called pride, a sense of feeling good about yourself.

And when people find out about your accomplishment, they are going to feel good about you, too.

The Mental Edge
~Revised

The Mind

To think that I am not going
To think of you anymore
Is still thinking of you
Let me then try not to think
That I am not going to think of you

I named my martial arts school Mushin Martial Arts over 20 years ago, after reading about Takuan, a Japanese zen master and swordsman who lived hundreds of years ago. I liked the concept of mushin, and I adapted it to the American freestyle fighting approach that I taught then, and still teach today. Although I said in the introduction that this book is an American approach to using the mind in the martial arts, I have included the Japanese concept of mushin here for one reasons– it works and is easily adaptable to our American ways.

Mushin (pronounced moo-shin) literally translated means, no-mind, or non-abiding mind. This is what Takuan said about it. "To speak in terms of your military art: If you see in a glance your opponent's striking sword and think, I'll block him there, your mind will get stuck on your opponent's sword, the motion will go out of your swordplay and you will be cut down. This is what may be called, stopping."

You probably know that many of today's fighting arts came

from observing the fighting and survival tactics of animals and insects. For example, Shaolin monks studied and emulated the movements of the preying mantis, white crane, monkey and tiger, and named their systems after them, such as White Crane style and Preying Mantis style. The monks discovered that the physical techniques were great, but when it came to using the mind, there was a big difference between man and beast: Man could reason, which had its good and bad.

What was good was that humans could plot their attacks and counter-attacks. What was bad was that they would fix their minds on some element of their opponent, like a weapon or a particular fighting trait. When this happened, it would leave them vulnerable to surprise attacks. The monks also found that they couldn't initiate an attack with complete freedom because their minds were stuck on whether their opponent would kick or punch in response.

They grew to realize that when their mind focused on one thing, they were left vulnerable, and since they were fighting for their lives rather than plastic trophies, they had to devise a way to keep their minds flowing during battle. The Chinese called what they found Wu-shin. We will continue to use the Japanese word, mushin.

Let's begin our discussion of mushin with a dramatic illustration, a sort of Jackie Chan-type fight in which an expert finds himself surrounded by five attackers. As the brawl begins, the mind of our expert remains calm as his eyes take in information: five men, one holding a knife, one well over six feet tall and about 240 pounds, one very drunk, one frightened, and one barking out orders to the others.

Our expert remains serene, his heart rate and breathing elevated only slightly. But there is something odd about his eyes: They don't appear to be looking directly at the attackers, but rather gazing at them, almost as if he were looking off in the distance. The tall, 240-pound man charges first.

The expert's rear leg lifts, hooks, and his heel slams into the man's square jaw. But before he hits the pavement, the knife fighter leaps forward with a glimmering slash. In an instant, his arm is caught by the expert and his elbow breaks with a loud pop that sounds like a fired 22- round.

Our expert spins away from the screaming man and drives a powerful sidekick into the ample mid-section of the drunk, who drops hard onto the pavement. The ringleader shouts desperately for the remaining man to charge, but the expert's piercing gaze and odd calm hypnotically holds the frightened man motionless. A moment later, he turns and runs off.

There is an aura of quiet around the expert as he stands motionless, not focusing on, but aware of the fallen men and the standing leader. The expert's thoughts are not on what he had done or on what might yet happen. His mind is like an undisturbed lake, only reflecting what is.

The ringleader starts to advance, but one of his fallen buddies coughs and moans. The leader's eyes dart from the expert to the three lying on the ground. He swallows hard and looks back to the expressionless face of the man responsible. A few seconds pass, and the leader does an about face and runs off in the direction of the coward.

Though surrounded, he remains calm. He doesn't concentrate on any one attacker, but he's aware of them all.

Our expert was able to dispatch the attackers because of where his mind was and where it wasn't. Let me clarify this statement before you accuse me of being one of those phony baloney teachers spouting nonsensical garbage I talked about in the introduction.

All of the attackers had dangerous characteristics. One was large and powerful, another was armed, one's courage was fortified with booze, one was a coward, and one was the leader. If we held a roundtable discussion with five other experts in the martial arts as to how they would defend themselves in such a situation, we would probably get at least three, maybe even five different approaches. One expert would deal with the knife first, another would argue that it would be best to take out the leader right away, while another expert would say he would knock down the biggest man to demoralize the others.

But our expert didn't plan anything. He saw the danger surrounding him, noted the dangers that each of the attackers brought to the party, but his brain didn't stick on KNIFE! or BIG GUY! He kept his eyes open and his mind clear of preconceived possibilities of attacks and defense. His mind simply flowed, continually taking everything in, but without stopping on any one thing in particular.

This is how Takuan said it way back then. "...the mind moves in response to the [five] men [five] times, and if the mind does not dwell on any of them, you will move and confront them one after another, and there will be no trace of inadequacy. However, if you stop the mind and face only one man, you may be able to deal with him, but you will surely fail with the next man."

This is what Bruce Lee said about mushin. "Concentration in Kung fu does not have the usual sense of restricting the attention to a single object, but is simply a quiet awareness of whatever happens to be here and now. Such concentration can be illustrated by an audience at a football game: Instead of a concentrated attention on the player who has the ball, they have an awareness of the whole football field. In a similar way, a gung fu man's mind is concentrated by not dwelling on any particular part of the opponent. This is especially true when dealing with many opponents."

Your Mind Should Flow

The ideal state of your mind in battle, the state of mushin, is that it flows continuously, not pausing to note detail, or to be concerned, or frightened, or to reason. It just perceives and flows, naturally and unconsciously. Our expert fought that way. He only dealt with what was presented to him at a given instant in time, then flowed on to the next instant and to whatever was happening then.

If it were you fighting those five attackers, and your mind was cluttered with thoughts and anticipation of being clobbered by that 240-pound man or stabbed by the man with the knife, you would have a hard time reacting spontaneously. As soon as your mind locked on the blade, the intoxicated man could whack you from behind. As soon as you decided to take out the leader, the knife fighter would slice through your ribs. When your mind stops, it's no longer free to react.

There is a samurai saying that goes like this: "If you look at your opponent's sword you will be killed by it." In other words, if your concentration is so focused on your opponent's weapon, be it a fist, foot or a knife, you won't be able to see all of his potential as well as any threats from others. Sometimes this is called tunnel vision, because it's like looking through a tunnel and seeing only what is revealed in that little hole. There may be lots of threats outside that hole, but you can see only what it reveals.

When You Spar

Let's see how mushin relates to your sparring with, Susan, a classmate of equal rank to yours. She has a particularly fast and powerful roundhouse kick that you are all too familiar with since she has hit you with it before, as well as other students. You begin the session anticipating her kick, planning to cleverly side step it and kick her with a roundhouse of your own.

As you begin sparring, you wait and watch for that kick of hers. You shuffle around, giddy with anticipation as to how you are going to move aside and punish her with your counter. Suddenly, she leaps forward with a mighty shout and slams a ridge hand strike into the side of your neck. Oookaaay, so she caught

115

The victim is so concentrated on the knife-

that he is unable to see or defend against the kick.

you by surprise that time. You move around again, ever watchful of that killer kick of hers, but again she scores on you, this time with a backfist. This is starting not to be fun anymore, but it will continue to happen since your mind is not open and free of other possibilities. It's stopped on just one thing and closed to everything else.

This can also happen when it's you who possesses the killer technique, say a reverse punch that could knock over a mule. You stalk your opponent ready to show her, and everyone else who is lucky enough to be watching, just how awesome your technique is. Your plan is to explode forward and punch her as fast as a streaking lightning bolt. What happens, though, is that every time you go to make your move, your opponent hits you first with a kick or a punch. In fact, the more you think and plan about delivering your technique, the more he hits you.

The Exercises

Below are some things you can incorporate into your regular training that will help you experience mushin. Don't get frustrated if you find that you are like the perplexed lover in the poem at the beginning of this chapter, who finds that it's tough to not think about not thinking of his lover. With mushin, the harder you try to think about not thinking about what you are doing, the more you think about it. But with continual practice, you will happily discover that you can attack, block and counterattack without giving a moments thought.

Begin by using your opponent's shoulder/chin area as your primary focus point. Use your eyes to gaze– not look– as if you were gazing through him at something off in the distance. The samurai called this "Fixing one's eyes on the far mountains." Don't let your eyes focus on any one thing, but rather be aware of your opponent in his totality: his head, arms and legs. You can see all of these things from the focus point.

Gaze through your opponent as you await his attack or for an opening in his defense. When you are attacked, block quickly; when an opening appears, attack it hard and fast. Give the moment only brief attention and then let your mind clear and be ready for whatever happens next. Here is how you shouldn't think.

Don't react to an attack by thinking, "Yipes! A kick is coming at me. I think I'll sidestep and block it with my left hand and then–" or when you see an opening appear in your opponent's defense, don't go, "Yippee! An opening. I'm going to sidekick it with my right foot." In these situations, your mind has stopped and lingered while you made your decision. Meanwhile, your opponent's kick found the mark, and his opening disappeared. In addition to missing an opportunity, your fixed mind is also susceptible to being faked. Your opponent can easily slip in another technique or two while your mind is still fixed on the initial attack. In the next chapter, we will discuss ways you can use your opponent's fixed mind to your advantage.

OK, back to how you *should* be thinking. When your mind is not anticipating or overreacting to anything, it will simply react to your opponent's initial attack and then continue flowing as it monitors whatever happens next. When your opponent launches a backfist at you, your brain will acknowledge the moment, send a defensive response to your muscles to block or evade, then immediately clear and again flow. If the backfist is a fake, your mind won't be stopped by it. It will deal with it only for the duration it exists, then be ready for whatever happens next. A mushin mind is harder to fake.

Mushin Reaction Drill I

When you are just learning to experience mushin, you need to be in an environment that is quiet; it's hard to experience it if you are in a noisy atmosphere, such as one with rowdy students or loud rock music. Also, your muscles need to be relaxed and your mind must be calm and void of any anticipation. There is no competition in this drill, so there is no anxiety over winning, losing or looking bad.

Face your partner and gaze calmly at his shoulder/chin area as he launches a *slow* backfist. Since your mind is calm and clear, you perceive the fist and easily block it, and then your mind instantly clears and is ready for whatever happens next.

This time it's your turn, and you throw a *slow* straight punch to your opponent's mid-section. His clear mind easily sees the punch, he blocks it and he is ready for whatever happens next.

You will both continue this exchange, making sure to clear your minds after each technique.

Your long-term goal in the exercise is to increase the speed of your techniques, although you shouldn't be overanxious to get to that level. It's far more important for your development of mushin that you first develop control over your mind and body before you start slamming home fast and furious techniques. You won't develop mushin if you move to the advanced level too quickly, and the drill will end up being no different than any other.

When I first taught this several years ago, I was pleasantly surprised to discover that even those students with only a few months of training easily caught on to the exercise. All of the students were impressed with how quickly they could respond to random attacks as long as they were able to maintain minds that were calm and unencumbered. They also noted that the opposite was true: If their minds became distracted, such as looking at another classmate, or glancing at the clock, they could not block and counter attack as well.

Mushin Reaction Drill II

You need two training partners to work with you on this drill. Don't advance to this exercise until you feel you have a good grasp of Mushin Reaction Drill I.

Begin by designating one person as the defender (you, in this case) and the other two as attackers. Again, everyone needs to be mentally and physically relaxed in order to benefit from the drill's objective. Once everyone is ready, the first student will launch a medium-speed backfist, followed a second later by the second student throwing a medium-speed roundhouse punch. The more clear and unencumbered your mind, the more easily you can block the first attack and flow right into blocking the second. Repeat this several times, and then rotate the role of defender.

As you get increasingly competent, which could take from three to six sessions depending on how able you are to relax and maintain a calm mind, you will find that you can maintain your skill even as you begin to slowly increase the speed of your techniques. If you experience problems, it's generally a result of your mind becoming cluttered with thoughts or distracted by things going on around you. If it happens, don't become frustrated or angry at yourself, because that places too much attention on the distraction. Just let the stray thought pass, and then clear your mind and continue with the exercise.

In the beginning, you need to practice these drills in quiet, so you may want to do them with as few students as possible. However, I've taught them successfully to a class of over 20 students, and we had success because everyone remained quiet. Don't allow radios or observers in the class during these drills. If you find that you or your partner are getting distracted or otherwise losing concentration, stop, resume your relaxation exercises and start over.

Without argument, this is an unrealistic environment, but this is a new concept, a new drill, one that requires maximum concentration not to think. In time, you will be able to experience mushin in any environment, but like most things, you have to start at the beginning.

Mushin in its purest form happens without conscious thought, or at the most, a minimum of thought, given to your opponent or yourself. You are ready and able to act, but you have no specific techniques in mind, and you make no judgements about what may or may not happen. Your blocking and attacking are done fluidly, directed by your subconscious mind as a result of your training in physical techniques and mental relaxation exercises.

Bruce Lee called mushin "it." Once he was asked how he would fight if he had to defend his life, he replied that he would hurt the assailant badly, possibly kill him. He said that if he would have to stand trial, he would say that he was not responsible for what he did, because he would have acted without conscious thought. He would tell the judge that "it" killed the attacker, not him. Bruce Lee clearly understood mushin and it's significance to fighting freely.

(However, as an ex-cop, let me tell you that his excuse to the judge would have been laughed at, and he would have found himself behind bars.)

The Mental

Edge

~Revised

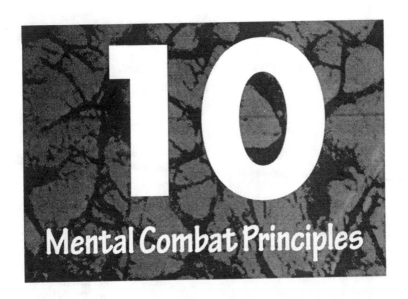

10
Mental Combat Principles

So far we have been talking about your mind in the martial arts. Now let's look at some ways to affect your opponent's mind, whether in competition, or in some dark, dank alley. You have heard instructors and fellow students say that all things being equal, the winner of a fight will be the fighter with the best endurance, or the best initial move, or the best footwork, or the best defense, or best something else. I say the fighter who can manipulate his opponent's mind, that is, his thinking process, will be the victor. All it takes is an understanding of basic fighting principles.

Principles are rules, or as Webster's dictionary defines the word, "basic truths;" I call them "absolutes" since they can't be changed. A principle you are familiar with is one called gravity. When you throw a ball into the air, gravity will pull it right back down again. You can't change this principle, but you can change the technique you use to throw the ball up: You can throw it underhand, overhand, over your back and through your legs. The same is true with fighting principles. You can change the techniques, but you can't change the principles.

While many people in the fighting arts use the word principle generically when referring to different elements of fighting, there are really only a few. We are going to look at two here and see how your understanding of them can give you an advantage in a fight.

THE DISTRACTION PRINCIPLE

The mind can only think of one thing at a time, and that is what the distraction principle is based on. While the mind can shift focus quickly, it still needs a split second of time to make the change. With your understanding of the distraction principle and your ability to use it against your opponent, a split second is all you need.

Here is an example of how the mind can be slowed. Say a fellow student walks up to you and whips an arnis stick into your shin. You yelp a few choice words, leap up and down on your good leg, and grab at your injured one. The pain is absolutely excruciating and you feel a wave of nausea in your stomach as your eyes tear up. All of your attention is focused on that little spot that is rapidly swelling and emanating horrible pain. At this exact moment, another student calmly says "Catch" and tosses you a tennis ball.

The chances are quite high that you are not going to catch it. Most likely it will bounce off your forehead, though you will be too busy hopping and yelping to notice. If you have ever slammed your shin into something hard or been struck hard there in your training, you know what I'm talking about. There is just no way you are going to shift your mind from that hot spot on your shin to catching a ball.

While you may not always have an arnis stick on you, you can use the principle of distraction in other ways, even ways less severe than bashing your opponent's vulnerable shin bone. The idea is to direct your opponent's brain to go where *you* want it to.

The most common form of distraction is to fake. It's a simple concept, one that creates a belief that a specific attack or movement is happening, while in reality the real technique is coming a second or two later. When you thrust your palm toward your opponent's face, he thinks, if only for a second, that his face is going to get struck. He reacts by trying to block it or by moving out of the way. It's at that moment of distraction when you drive a hard kick between his legs.

When the fake is executed correctly, you put into motion several things in your opponent's mind. First, his eyes see the palm and then they send a signal to his brain, "Warning! Warning!"

A fake is a partial technique that looks real enough to distract your opponent's mind–

so that you can drive home a completed technique.

which quickly computes the message to "Yipes! an incoming palm! I better do something!" His brain then chooses from any number of responses–block, duck, side step, run–and then sends the choice to the appropriate muscles. It's when all this is going on that you fire off your second technique, the one you want to land.

Processing of the information takes only a tiny part of a second, but when your second technique is timed just right, his brain must interrupt the processing in order to process the new information. But since it just can't make the switch fast enough, your second blow slams home. To put it into a neat package, here are three reasons your second technique will score.

* Your fake is so convincing that your opponent's attention remains fixed on it, and he fails to see the second attack.
* The second technique disrupts his mental processing of the fake, but he hasn't completely recognized the second technique as an actual threat.
* He recognizes the second attack as a threat, but his mind hasn't sent the appropriate reaction to his muscles.

When a fake doesn't work, it's because it doesn't look real to your opponent. Keep in mind that a fake is a partial technique, but enough of one to fool your opponent into reacting to it. If his mind doesn't believe it, he won't respond.

It is important to keep in mind that a significant percentage of street assailants are acting under the influence of alcohol. A drunk has difficulty seeing and responding to a fake, because his vision, and his ability to think clearly and to get his muscles moving are all impaired from the depressant. This doesn't mean you can't fake him, but you might have to modify your usual fake a little. One way is to simply throw it a little slower than you normally would, so that the drunk can see it and register it in his pickled brain. Another way is to throw it so it blocks his vision. A good example is a palm fake to the face, holding it there an instant longer than normal to get his attention, and briefly cover his field of vision. You then take advantage of the distraction and drive your other fist into any exposed target. It's sort of a win/win deal: He gets lots of time to see your fake, and you get extra time to punch him out.

You can also try a sacrifice blow. This is similar to a fake except you want your opponent to go ahead and block your technique. This wouldn't be a good thing to do against a fighter who you know has a fast counter punch. But if he is the kind who blocks frequently without countering, go ahead and sacrifice a low kick to tie up his mind and hands, then blast him with a head punch.

Distracting For Grappling

Police defensive tactics falls under the heading of grappling, along with jujitsu, chin-na, aikido and wrestling. Using the principle of distracting saved my bacon as a police officer many times. Virtually everyone I arrested didn't want to be, and some put up a fuss, sometimes a considerable fuss. I quickly learned as a cop, that people in real life don't just stand by as you take their arm and apply a wrist lock or a leg sweep. They move around evasively, stiffen their arm if you do get hold of it, then punch you in the nose as you struggle to twist their wrist. I found by studying in the school of hard knocks, that when I attacked with a grappling technique against someone who didn't want me too, I needed to first move his mind someplace other than where I was going to grab.

Here is one of my favorite concepts.

Softening

A "softening" technique is a hand strike, kick, pinch, head butt or any other device used to distract an opponent from your intended grappling technique. An extreme example is to kick a guy in the groin to get him thinking about that target, then you move in and apply an armbar.

In the last few years, jujitsu has grown in popularity among people who previously trained only in the punching and kicking arts. Initially, karate people wondered how you could grab a wrist when it was attached to a speeding backfist. While there are sone jujitsu masters who can do it, the rest of us have to rely on distraction techniques, like softening.

Nothing softens up a guy like a quick kick to the groin.

Then grab his arm–

–and apply a knuckle press into his ulna nerve.

This time you block and catch his flailing arm–

soften him with a not-so-soft whack in the groin–

and finish with a hand twist.

When your opponent throws a punch, his thought process is divided between his punch and its intended target. When you swat his punch aside and slap your foot between his legs, his entire attention is focused on his groin. Even if your kick misses and strikes his thigh, his attention is distracted just enough for you to apply a grappling technique. Don't believe it? Have your training partner kick you in the cookies and see where your thought process goes. It's definitely not on the wrist he's grabbing.

There are basically two types of grappling techniques: those that affect pain and those that rely on leverage. Those that cause pain have a point that I call lock-in, a place where the technique has placed the joint, tendon, and muscles at its most extreme. It's a place where the pain is excruciating and near impossible to escape from, at least not without causing serious injury. With most techniques, there is little or no pain before the lock-in takes place. Therefore, when you first grab the arm and until you get to the lock-in, you are likely to get resistance from your opponent. This can quickly turn into a muscle contest, and if you are not the strongest person, you lose.

You don't want this to happen, and it won't if you understand his thinking process. Say you have grabbed his arm with the intention of bending it at the elbow and applying a wrist lock, a common control technique in police defensive tactics. Just as you begin to bend it, he clenches his fist and tenses his arm muscles, which prevents you from getting to the lock-in. At this point, his thought process is on his stiff arm and on trying to keep you from hurting him. The more you struggle to gain control, the more he tenses and the greater his mental focus. Any cop will tell you that this is a common way to resist this technique.

Since you are getting nowhere quick struggling with him, you need to redirect his attention from his arm to another point. I like to call this softening technique a "crab bite," because it's subtle, it hurts like the dickens, and it feels like, well, a crab bite. When you feel your opponent's arm tense up, use the fingernails of your thumb and index finger of your closest hand to pinch the soft flesh inside his upper arm. When he reacts to the

When you "crab bite" a guy's eyelid (pinch a little tender skin with the nails of your thumb and index finger), he will follow you anywhere.

acute pain, you immediately use your same hand to strike against the inside of his elbow to bend his arm. His arm will bend because his mental focus has diverted from keeping it stiff, to where there is a sensation of having his tender flesh torn. This distraction is only momentary, so you must make your move quickly before he refocuses his mind and strength.

Here is a variation. Say you have locked-in the wrist hold, but because you are both sweaty or he doesn't feel the pain (I hate guys who don't feel pain), your opponent starts to get out of it. As he struggles to free himself from your grip, you must divert his attention, so you can regain the hold or flow into another one. A crab bite works great in this situation.

When Someone Grabs You

Distraction also works when someone has grabbed your clothing, has a grappling hold on you, or his hand is frozen on a gun or knife. As in the last scenario, the harder you try to release his grip, the more he focuses mentally on maintaining it. When his strength is focused, especially if he is mentally ill or over-the-top enraged, his power can be extraordinary. Crab bites and groin kicking are good distraction and softening techniques to use when you are grabbed. Here are some others.

• Grab your person's neck cord with your thumb and index finger and twist and pinch.

When you reach deep into a tackler's hair and twist hard, his thoughts will be on his scalp, not on your legs.

• Push your thumb or flick a finger against the outside corner of the person's eye. If the situation warrants it, consider going directly into his eye.

• Grab the sides, top or back of the person's hair, close your fingers tightly against his scalp, and twist hard to the left or right.

I've used the neck cord twist many times against motorists, usually drunk drivers who were gripping the steering wheel in a death grip and refusing to let go. I'd reach in and pin their left hand against the steering wheel, so they couldn't offer me a fist sandwich, then I'd grab a neck cord and twist it as I simultaneously jerked their hand free. I would then apply a wrist lock and guide the "gentleman" out the car door.

When I worked skid row, a favorite technique of fallen winos was to grab my legs and try to pull me down. Since it's hard and awkward to pull someone's arms away from you in that position, I'd go for a distraction by flicking my finger against the outside of the guy's eye. Since everyone is protective and squeamish of their eyes, this would startle him enough to enable me to free my legs.

I love hair techniques because they are excruciatingly painful, and give clear direction as to what you want the person to do. I used them many times as takedown techniques, pain compliance holds, and as a way to distract.

I walked into a family fight one time where the boyfriend was trying to crush his girlfriend's baby. A couple of other officers were punching the guy in the head, but that only made the creep crush the baby even more intensely. So I quickly thrust my hand to the back of the guy's head, grabbed a fistful of hair all the way to his scalp, and twisted as far and as hard as I could. When the man screamed and jerked his hands toward his head, one of the other officers grabbed the baby. Then I used the hair technique to soften the guy enough, so that I could apply a joint lock on his arm and put on the handcuffs.

High/Low
The high/low approach to distracting is another favorite of mine. As we have been talking about all along, the distraction

Force an attacker's attention low by kicking his inside knee–

and then follow with a high technique, such as a gouge to both of his eyes.

principle relies on the fact that the brain can only think of one thing at a time, and when you divert your opponent's mind from point A to point B, you give yourself an edge in the fight. High/low also moves the opponent's brain, but moves it a greater distance than what we have been talking about so far. You will use high/low when you want your opponent to think extremely high while you attack extremely low, or vice versa.

A good example would be a low roundhouse kick to your opponent's calf followed by a snapping backfist to his ear. What happens is that his attention first gets diverted to your kick when you launch it, and stays focused on your kick as it slams painfully into his leg. At this moment, he isn't thinking about his stance, his guard, his new car, or his girlfriend. His brain, and possibly his eyes, are focused low where your foot is causing pain to the tender muscles of his calf. It's at that moment that you snap a backfist against his ear.

You can fake low or high and get the same reaction from your opponent. In a street fight, you can fake a low snap kick toward your opponent's shin, and when he reacts to it by moving his leg out of the way or swatting at it, you quickly thrust a finger into his eye. Since most karate tournaments don't allow leg kicks or even fakes to the legs, you have to raise the low fake to groin level, and then strike high for the point. A double roundhouse kick– low then high– works perfectly for this and is quite popular in tournaments, as is kicking high to the opponent's head, then sweeping his legs out from under him when he goes for the block. Whether you are hitting or faking with your first technique, your objective is to move your opponent's mind in the opposite direction of where you intend to hit.

Throwing Multiple High/Low Hits

When you hit high, low, high, then low again, you can really mess up your opponent's mind. This is because after two or three of these opposite-end hits, his mind can't catch up to what you are doing. When your kick connects with his knee, his thought process races down to that place, and then a split second later, when your backfist whacks into his head, his mind races up to that point. But just as the pain of that blow registers, you throw another low kick into his calf, and then as his now sluggish mind reluctantly starts moving toward his lower leg, you add a cherry on the pudding with a ridge hand across his nose.

It's hard enough for your training partner to respond well to a high/low barrage when the techniques are being pulled. Imagine what a street thug, especially one who is not trained, thinks when you overwhelm him with blows that cause pain.

ACTION/REACTION PRINCIPLE

Even if you haven't heard of the action/reaction principle, you have, nonetheless, used it and had it used against you. This principle states that action is faster than reaction or, said another way, reaction is slower than action. For example when you stand within striking range of that beer-gutted tavern junkie, your chance of getting hit, no matter how many stripes you have on your black belt, is extremely high. I conducted an informal study one year of police officers who had been punched, pushed, kicked and stabbed. In every case, the officer was standing within striking range of the suspect when the assault occurred.

When you are standing within striking range of someone and they decide to hit you, you have no idea of his decision until you see his punch rushing toward your face. He decides when to do it and how to do it, all while you stand there innocent as a newborn lamb. Since he is standing close enough to hit you, he doesn't have to take a forward step, a move that usually hints that something is about to happen. He gives no warning, and now you have to react to the sudden action. First, your eyes must send a message to your brain that you are in danger from an incoming fist. Your brain must digest the information from your eyes and decide what to do about it, either block, duck, or scream. But since you were so close to the attack, your reaction is too late. His fist snaps your head back, and you get a blurry look at the ceiling as you crash to the floor.

Rooster Fighting

Having patrolled a beat in skid row where I daily checked out some of the toughest drinkin' joints around, I saw a lot of fights erupt. It's amazing how many start out with the two com-

Never allow a threatening person to get this close. It's next to impossible to react in time if he should throw a punch.

batants doing a thing I call Rooster Fighting. No doubt you have seen it, too. It happens when two riled up guys stand inflated chest to inflated chest, cursing, challenging, baiting each other to swing. It's done so much in the world of macho fighting, that it's almost as if it's some mandatory, ritualistic prelude. At the peak of the posturing, the chests bump once or several times, then someone swings, and if he doesn't over do it and fall down, the blow lands.

This is crazy, and you should never ever do this or let some- one do it to you. If a confrontation is brewing, stay at least an arm's reach away from the guy, more if you have a hint that he might be a kicker. You need time to see, perceive, and respond to his move. Do it for your brain, and ultimately do it for your flesh and bones.

You also want to stay out of range when you are sparring in your school or in competition. Many fighters believe that the person who attacks first usually scores. Well, that may or may not be true, though it's just about a guarantee if the two fighters are squared off within range of each other. Never begin your competition with your lead hand touching your opponent's lead hand. That may have looked cool when Bruce Lee did it with Bob Wall in *Enter The Dragon*, but in reality, you are teaching yourself a bad habit, one that could spread to the street where opponents use knives and bottles.

Here's the rub. When you are standing out of range from your training partner, competitor, or Bruno, the bar thug, you have to close the distance between you to land an attack. But you can do it because you diligently practice your footwork, fakes and other gap-closing moves. Right?

Stay Away From His Weapon

You know it's going to be a bad day on your underwear when someone confronts you with a gun. While there are lots of books and magazine articles that illustrate techniques against a gun, to be blunt, most of them offer utter nonsense. Those kicks and flips that look so thrilling in photos are secondary to getting your body out of the line of fire. If you don't accomplish that, your coolest techniques will go unseen.

Actually, you have two objectives when facing a gun: get yourself out of the bullet's path, and get your hand on the gun. To be successful, two things must occur: you must be close enough to the gun to touch it, and you must do something to slow the gunman's mental process. If you are not close enough, don't attempt a disarm. If you are absolutely convinced that he is going to shoot, then turn and run like crazy. Statistics show that shooters rarely hit a running target. If you are within touching range, though, and convinced he is going to shoot, then you should go for the disarm. To be successful, you must manipulate the guy's mind.

If he is talking to you, his mind is thinking about what he is saying. It's preferable for him to do the talking, but if he is the silent killer type, you need to occupy his mind with what you

Try to get the gunman to talk so that his mind is occupied on what he is saying and thus slow down his reaction to your movement.

Then twist quickly and grab the weapon.

are saying. You want to get his mind involved, so that it's slow to respond to your action. Notice that you have both principles working here: distraction and action/reaction.

When you feel his mind is sufficiently occupied on his words or on yours, make your move. Twist your body hard to the right or left to get out of the bullet's path, swat the gun aside, and keep hold of it. Do whatever follow-up techniques you choose as long as you keep hold of the weapon and weapon hand, and keep the gun pointed away from you.

The essential element when disarming is that you move when the gunman's mind is occupied, so that he has to stop his current thought process and move it to what you are doing. In other words, he has to react to your action.

● ● ● ● ●

To be a smart fighter, you need to understand why your techniques work. Concepts such as faking, angling, broken rhythm, jamming, counter punching and rushing all fall into one or both of the principles we have discussed. When you understand why your favorite technique or any technique works, you will be able to come up with even more techniques to apply to the principles.

When two people are equal physically, the smarter one, the fighter with greater knowledge about himself and his opponent's mind, will reign victorious.

LIFE IS HARD; IT'S HARDER WHEN YOU'RE STUPID

Notes

Other Books Available From Desert Publications